THE OFFICIAL
LIVERPOOL FC
SUPPORTER'S BOOK

First published in 2010
Reprinted with corrections in 2012
Second edition 2013

Copyright © Carlton Books Limited 2010, 2013

Carlton Books Limited
20 Mortimer Street
London W1T 3JW

A CIP catalogue record for this book is available from the British Library

ISBN 978-1-78097-339-5

Editor: Martin Corteel
Project art editor: Luke Griffin
Production: Janette Burgin

Printed and bound by CPI Group (UK) Ltd, Croydon, CR0 4YY

THE OFFICIAL
LIVERPOOL FC
SUPPORTER'S BOOK

JOHN WHITE

CARLTON
BOOKS

CONTENTS

INTRODUCTION

As every Reds fan knows, Liverpool FC is the greatest Club in the world. Since its formation in 1892, Liverpool has become a name synonymous with footballing class, skill and achievement. The Club has won 18 league titles, seven FA Cup finals, eight League Cup finals and 11 European trophies (including the European Cup/Champions League on five occasions) and has won over millions of fans in the process. In *The Official Liverpool Football Supporters' Book*, the reader will find everything any fan could want to know about his or her favourite club.

This book kicks off with a chapter of Liverpool facts and trivia, in which super stats and random factoids are intriguingly combined. Then, you can find reviews of Liverpool's championship and cup-winning campaigns, plus potted biographies of a host of Club legends, from Jamie Carragher and Kenny Dalglish to Bill Shankly and Phil Thompson. Classic European nights are also recalled, including the Reds' sensational Champions League triumph over AC Milan in Istanbul in 2005.

You can also delight in a chapter of Liverpool fantasy teams and a collection of memorable Liverpool quotes. Practise your vocals in our compilation of supporters' songs and chants, before testing your wits in the ultimate Liverpool supporters' quiz.

All in all, this is the perfect read for any dedicated Liverpool fan, which should intrigue, amaze and entertain all fans – much like the team has done on so many mega occasions. Enjoy!

CHAPTER 1

LIVERPOOL FACTS & TRIVIA

We all know that Liverpool Football Club, founded in 1892, has a glorious history and that some of the world's greatest players and managers have helped to make the Reds one of the best-loved and most respected of all football clubs on the planet.

Over the next pages you will discover hundreds of interesting facts and statistics about Liverpool, the players, the managers, the great matches and other moments which have shaped the Reds. If you wish, you can read through the whole section in one sitting, but this is not a running history and thus is ideal for dipping into and enjoying, a few nuggets at a time.

If you want to know which players were bought and sold in Liverpool's record transfer deals, or the club's complete European record, you'll find this information in these pages. There are also landmarks to recall, such as the first matches, first captains, first goals, first internationals, etc. Then there are other notable items, such as the first man to make 100 appearances in Europe, the scorer of the Reds' 1,000th Premier League goal, the passing of the armband as Liverpool club captain. The variety is both mind-boggling and very entertaining.

So, sit down, put on your red scarf and dream of the time when you are sitting at Anfield watching the champions of Europe flaying the opposition and a sea of Red friends joining you in celebration.

The Trophy Cabinet

League Division One champions (18 times)
1901, 1906, 1922, 1923, 1947, 1964, 1966, 1973, 1976, 1977,
1979, 1980, 1982, 1983, 1984, 1986, 1988, 1990

League Division Two champions (4 times)
1894, 1896, 1905, 1962

FA Cup winners (7 times)
1965, 1974, 1986, 1989, 1992, 2001, 2006

League Cup winners (record 8 times)
1981, 1982, 1983, 1984, 1995, 2001, 2003, 2012

FA Charity Shield winners (15 times)
1966, 1974, 1976, 1979, 1980, 1982, 1988, 1989, 2001, 2006
Joint winners: 1964, 1965, 1977, 1986, 1990

European Cup/Champions League winners (5 times)
1977, 1978, 1981, 1984, 2005

UEFA Cup winners (3 times) 1973, 1976, 2001

European Super Cup winners (3 times)
1977, 2001, 2005

Screen Sport Super Cup winners (1 occasion) 1986

Carlsberg Trophy winners (3 times)

Manager of the Year Awards (11 times)

Never too young nor too old

The youngest player to score a first-team goal for Liverpool was Michael Owen, who netted against Wimbledon on 6 May 1997, aged 17 years and 144 days. Billy Liddell is the club's oldest goalscorer netting against Stoke City on 5 March 1960, aged 38 years and 55 days.

In safe hands

Liverpool goalkeeper Pepe Reina won three consecutive Barclays Golden Gloves awards for the most clean sheets in a Premier League season, 2005–06 to 2007–08. He was denied a fourth award in 2009–10, when Petr Cech achieved the same 17 clean sheets but did so in fewer matches.

Reds match Toffees

Liverpool came back from 3–1 down against West Ham United in the 2006 FA Cup final at the Millennium Stadium Cardiff, to force extra time. The Reds won the trophy, 3–1 on penalties. Everton had been the last team to win the FA Cup after trailing by two goals. In 1966. The Toffees trailed Sheffield Wednesday 2–0 before winning 3–2 at Wembley,

DID YOU KNOW THAT?
Liverpool have won the UEFA Champions League, FA Cup, League Cup and FA Charity Shield, all in penalty shoot-outs.

Some famous Liverpool fans

Curtly Ambrose	cricketer
Johnny Ball	TV personality
Sue Barker	TV presenter
Ian Broudie	musician (Lightning Seeds)
Cilla Black	TV personality
Stan Boardman	comedian
Mel C	pop singer
Kelly Cates (née Dalglish)	TV presenter
Craig Charles	comedian and actor
Elvis Costello	musician
Chris de Burgh	musician
Dr Dre	rap artist
Kirsty Gallagher	TV presenter
Samuel L. Jackson	actor
Ian McCulloch	musician (Echo and the Bunnymen)
Mike Myers	actor
Peter Sissons	TV news presenter
Jimmy Tarbuck	comedian
Ricky Tomlinson	actor

Gerrard's quadruple

Steven Gerrard is the only player to score in the final of the FA Cup, League Cup, UEFA Cup and UEFA Champions League. He scored in the 2001 UEFA Cup Final against Alaves, 2003 League Cup Final against Manchester United, 2005 UEFA Champions League Final against AC Milan and 2006 FA Cup Final against West Ham United.

Quick off the mark

Robbie Fowler scored the fastest ever FA Premier League hat-trick when he bagged three against Arsenal at Anfield on 28 August 1994 in only 4 minutes and 33 seconds, just before the half-hour mark. Liverpool won the game 3–0.

England's Springbok Amateur

Gordon Hodgson was signed by the Reds in 1925 after he was spotted playing in South Africa. He was a prolific scorer, holding the club's goalscoring records until Roger Hunt arrived at the club. In 1930–31 he scored 36 goals, and in total he scored 240 goals in 378 games. He won three caps for England Amateurs at inside-right against Northern Ireland, Wales and Scotland in 1930 and 1931 while playing for Liverpool. He had already played for South Africa's amateur national team. Gordon Hodgson died in 1951.

World Club Championship

Liverpool have played in three FIFA World Club Championship finals and lost them all:

Date	Opposition (Country)	Venue	Result
13.12.1981	Flamengo (Brazil)	Tokyo	0–3
9.12.1984	Independiente (Argentina)	Tokyo	0–1
18.12.2005	Sao Paulo (Brazil)	Yokohama	0–1

Record transfers (paid)

The following table charts Liverpool's record transfer fees paid:

Player	Date	From	Fee
William Dunlop	Jan 1895	Abercorn	£35
Francis Becton	March 1895	Preston North End	£100
John Walker	April 1898	Heart of Midlothian	£350
Sam Hardy	May 1905	Chesterfield	£500
Fred Hopkin	May 1921	Manchester United	£2,800
Tom Morrison	Nov 1927	St Mirren	£4,000
Jim Smith	Sept 1929	Ayr United	£5,500
Tom Bradshaw	Jan 1930	Bury	£8,000
Albert Stubbins	Sept 1946	Newcastle United	£12,500
Kevin Lewis	June 1960	Sheffield United	£13,000
Gordon Milne	Aug 1960	Preston North End	£16,000
Ian St John	May 1961	Motherwell	£35,000
Peter Thompson	Aug 1963	Preston North End	£40,000
Emlyn Hughes	Feb 1967	Blackpool	£65,000
Tony Hateley	June 1967	Chelsea	£96,000
Alun Evans	Sept 1968	Wolverhampton W.	£100,000
John Toshack	Nov 1970	Cardiff City	£110,000
Ray Kennedy	July 1974	Arsenal	£180,000
David Johnson	Aug 1976	Ipswich Town	£200,000
Kenny Dalglish	Aug 1977	Celtic	£440,000
Craig Johnston	April 1981	Middlesbrough	£575,000
Mark Lawrenson	Aug 1981	Brighton & Hove A.	£900,000
Peter Beardsley	July 1987	Newcastle United	£1,900,000
Ian Rush	Aug 1988	Juventus	£2,800,000
Dean Saunders	July 1991	Derby County	£2,900,000
Phil Babb	Sept 1994	Coventry City	£3,600,000
Stan Collymore	July 1995	Nottingham Forest	£8,500,000
Emile Heskey	March 2000	Leicester City	£11,000,000
Djibril Cisse	July 2004	Auxerre	£14,000,000
Fernando Torres	July 2007	Atletico Madrid	£20,200,000
Luis Suarez	Jan 2011	Ajax	£22,800,000
Andy Carroll	Jan 2011	Newcastle United	£35,000,000

Hat-trick sub

Steve Staunton is the only Liverpool player to score a hat-trick after coming on as a substitute. He replaced Ian Rush against Wigan Athletic in the second leg of the League Cup second-round tie at Anfield on 4 October 1989. The Reds won 3–0, Staunton netting all three. Wigan chose to play their home leg at Anfield.

Party poopers

On 19 February 1910 Liverpool spoiled Manchester United's party by beating them 4–3 (Arthur Goddard and James Stewart both scored twice) in the first ever match at the newly built Old Trafford. Archibald Leitch, who designed Anfield, was also the architect of Old Trafford.

Norwegians put to the sword

On 17 September 1974, Stromsgodset visited Anfield in the first leg of the first round of the European Cup Winners' Cup. The Reds crushed the Norwegian amateur side 11–0 with every starting player, except for goalkeeper Ray Clemence and midfielder Brian Hall, appearing at least once on the scoresheet. Phil Boersma and Phil Thompson, two each, Alec Lindsay, Phil Neal, Tommy Smith, Peter Cormack, Emlyn Hughes, Steve Heighway, Ray Kennedy and Ian Callaghan got the goals in Liverpool's biggest ever victory.

Breaking the bank for Anfield stars

Liverpool players have always been highly prized and clubs have been willing to pay huge transfer fees for their services. The 12 biggest deals for Liverpool players are:

Player	Date	To	Fee
Fernando Torres	January 2011	Chelsea	£50.0m
Xabi Alonso	August 2009	Real Madrid	£30.0m
Javier Mascherano	August 2010	Barcelona	£17.25m
Robbie Fowler	November 2001	Leeds United	£12.5m
Raul Meireles	August 2011	Chelsea	£12.0m
Robbie Keane	February 2009	Tottenham Hotspur	£12.0m
Peter Crouch	July 2006	Portsmouth	£11.0m
Momo Sissoko	January 2008	Juventus	£8.2m
Michael Owen	August 2004	Real Madrid	£8.0m
Craig Bellamy	July 2007	West Ham United	£7.5m
Stan Collymore	February 2000	Aston Villa	£7m
Milan Baros	August 2005	Aston Villa	£6.5m

Stubbins honoured by Fab Four

Former Liverpool striker Albert Stubbins (1946–53), was honoured by the Beatles who included his image on the cover of their album *Sgt Pepper's Lonely Hearts Club Band.*

Liverpool employ a Digger

John Barnes is known as Digger, not because he had been a builder, but his full name is John Charles Barnes (JCB).

Liverpool robbed

In 1892–93, their first year in existence, Liverpool won the Lancashire League Championship. On 1 September 1893, the trophy was stolen from a pawnbroker's shop where it was on display. It was never recovered.

The great Dane

Joe Fagan brought Jan Molby to Anfield from Ajax Amsterdam in August 1984 for £200,000. Molby was one of many exciting up-and-coming players at Ajax, who included Marco van Basten, Frank Rijkaard and Jesper Olsen. Molby was a colossus in the heart of the Reds' midfield during his 12 years with the club. Although he was not the quickest of players, and sometimes struggled with his weight, his passing ability was second to none at the time. He made 291 appearances for the Reds, scoring 60 times, and won two First Division Championship winners' medals and two FA Cup winners' medals. In February 1996 Molby was appointed the player-manager of Swansea City.

Gerrard's Premier League hat-trick

Steven Gerrard netted his first ever Premier League hat-trick for Liverpool in a 5–0 hammering of Aston Villa at Anfield on 22 March 2009. Dirk Kuyt and Albert Riera scored the other goals.

Liverpool's first £1 million man

In July 1987 Peter Beardsley became the first player to cost Liverpool £1 million or more, when the club paid Newcastle United £1.9 million for his services, at the time a record fee between two British clubs.

World Soccer magazine awards

World Soccer magazine celebrated its 50th anniversary in 2010, but since 1982, it has named its player, manager and team of the year. Liverpool have received four awards: Michael Owen (*World Soccer* Player of the Year, 2001), Gerard Houllier (*World Soccer* Manager of the Year, 2001) and the club (*World Soccer* Team of the Year, 2001and 2005). In 1999, the magazine produced its *World Soccer* 100 Greatest Players of the Twentieth Century. Pele was No.1, but five Liverpool legends, Kenny Dalglish, 22, Ian Rush, 40, Michael Owen, 44, Kevin Keegan, 56, and Alan Hansen, 93, made the list.

Three Threes

Jack Balmer is the only player to score three consecutive hat-tricks for Liverpool. On 9 November 1946 the Reds beat Portsmouth 3–0 at Anfield; on 16 November they beat Derby County 4–1 at the Baseball Ground (Balmer netted all four); and on 23 November, Liverpool beat Arsenal 4–2 at Anfield (Albert Stubbins scored the other goal).

Reds keep the Cup

When Liverpool beat AC Milan on penalties to win the UEFA Champions League in 2005, they became the third team to win the trophy on five occasions, following Real Madrid and AC Milan. UEFA awarded the Champions League trophy to Liverpool in perpetuity and ordered the creation of a new trophy for the 2005–06 season. Two other clubs, in addition to Real, AC Milan and Liverpool, have received the honour, Bayern Munich and Ajax.

European Footballer of the Year

Michael Owen is the only Liverpool player to receive the *Ballon d'Or* as European Footballer of the Year whilst with the Reds. However, a number of other players finished in the top three in the voting, either with the club or at another time in their career. This is the full list

Year	Rank	Player	Nationality	Club
1977	Second	**Kevin Keegan**	English	Hamburg
1978	First	**Kevin Keegan**	English	Hamburg
1979	First	**Kevin Keegan**	English	Hamburg
1983	Second	**Kenny Dalglish**	Scottish	**Liverpool**
1995	Second	**Jari Litmanen**	Finnish	Ajax
2005	Third	**Steven Gerrard**	English	**Liverpool**
2008	Third	**Fernando Torres**	Spanish	**Liverpool**

DID YOU KNOW THAT?
Australian international Harry Kewell was Oceania Footballer of the Year when he was a Liverpool player in 2003.

Medallion man

Not only is Kenny Dalglish, MBE, the only player to have won all three domestic competitions in both England and Scotland, he was also the first to player score 100 goals in both English and Scottish Leagues. These are Kenny's major medals, won as a player or manager:

The Player

Celtic
Scottish Championship winner
1971–72, 1972–73, 1973–74, 1976–77
Scottish Cup winner
1971–72, 1973–74, 1975–75, 1976–77
Scottish League Cup winner
1974–75

Liverpool
League Championship winner
1978–79, 1979–80, 1981–82, 1982–83, 1983–84, 1985–86*, 1987–88*
FA Cup winner
1986*
League Cup winner
1980–81, 1981–82, 1982–83, 1983–84
European Cup winner
1977–78, 1980–81, 1983–84
European Super Cup winner
1977

* = won as Player-manager

The Manager

Liverpool
League Championship winner
1985–86*, 1987–88*, 1989–90
FA Cup winner
1986*, 1989
League Cup winner
2012

Blackburn Rovers
FA Premier League winner
1994–95

Celtic (caretaker manager)
Scottish League Cup winner
2000

Awards
PFA Player of the Year 1983
FWA Footballer of the Year
1979, 1983

England Football Hall of Fame
Scotland Football Hall of Fame

Member of the FIFA 100
Freedom of the City of Glasgow 1986

Call the doc

During his Liverpool days David Johnson was nicknamed "Doc" by his team-mates because he had a habit of carrying a bag that contained just about every type of cream and pill imaginable.

The Club Crest

The Club Crest is dominated by the Liver Bird, an imaginary cross between a cormorant and an eagle. When King John recognised Liverpool as a borough in 1207 (it was granted city status in 1880), an impression of the bird was incorporated into the wax that sealed the charter. Above the Liver Bird is the phrase, "You'll Never Walk Alone", originally a song in the 1945 Richard Rodgers & Oscar Hammerstein musical *Carousel*, but which in the 1960s became the anthem of Liverpool fans (especially on the Kop) – the words are also contained within the iron curlicues of the Shankly Gates. At the foot of the crest "EST. 1892" signifies the year of the club's formation. The flames were added following the 1989 Hillsborough disaster, in lasting memory of the 96 Liverpool fans who died in the tragedy.

Most loyal servant

Liverpool's longest-serving player was goalkeeper Elisha Scott, who was with the club for 21 years and 52 days, from 1913 to 1934. He made 468 appearances for the Reds

Nicknames

Here are some famous nicknames of Liverpool personnel:

John Barnes	**Digger**	Henry Lewis	**Harry**
Thomas Bradshaw	**Tiny**	Jason McAteer	**Dave**
Aboubacar Camara	**Titi**	William McConnell	**Billy Mac**
Harry Chambers	**Sharky/Smiler**	Steve McManaman	**Shaggy**
Kenny Dalglish	**King Kenny**	Ronnie Moran	**Bugsy**
Peter Crouch	**Coathanger**	Phil Neal	**Zico**
J Edward Doig	**Ned**	Steve Nicol	**Chico**
David Fairclough	**Supersub**	Berry Nieuwenhuys	**Nivvy**
Dietmar Hamann	**Didi**	Ronald Orr	**Wee**
Alan Hansen	**Jockey**	Bob Paisley	**Gunner**
Emlyn Hughes	**Crazy Horse**	Fred Rodgers	**The Bullet**
Robbie Fowler	**God**	Ronny Rosenthal	**Rocket**
Adolf Hanson	**Alf**	Neil Ruddock	**Razor**
Fred Hopkin	**Polly**	Ian Rush	**Omar**
John Hughes	**Geezer**	Ian St John	**Saint**
John Hunter	**Sailor**	John Scales	**Bond**
James Jackson	**The Parson**	Bill Shankly	**Shanks**
David Johnson	**Doc**	Steve Staunton	**Stan**
Thomas Johnson	**Tosh**	Graeme Souness	**Charlie**
Rob Jones	**Trigger**	Fernando Torres	**El Nino**
Alan Kennedy	**Barney Rubble**	Ron Yeats	**Rowdy**

The start of a long rivalry

The first Anfield derby against Everton was played on 17 November 1894. It ended in a 2–2 draw, with Jimmy Ross and David Hannah on getting the Liverpool goals.

Spurs manager was a Red

Keith Burkinshaw, who managed Tottenham Hotspur to FA Cup wins in 1981 and 1982 and to UEFA Cup success in 1984, made one appearance for the Reds during the 1954–55 season. In 1982 he became the only former Liverpool player to lead a team out against the Reds at Wembley, when Liverpool met Tottenham Hotspur in the League Cup final. That day, the Reds came out on top, winning 3–1 (Ronnie Whelan 2, Ian Rush).

Kop see FA Cup for the first time

On 4 May 1965, three days after lifting the FA Cup for the first time with the 2–1 extra time defeat of Leeds United at Wembley, Liverpool paraded the trophy in front of the Kop prior to the first leg of their European Cup semi-final against Inter Milan. Although the Reds beat Inter 3–1 at Anfield, they controversially lost the second leg 3–0

First ever League goalscorer

On 2 September 1893 Malcolm McVean scored Liverpool's first ever Football League goal. It came in the 2–0 away win at Middlesbrough Ironopolis, with Joe McQue slotting the other. An original member of the "Team of the Macs", McVean was signed from Third Lanark in 1892 and made 126 appearances for the club, scoring 40 goals.

Super Cup success

UEFA recognized the European Super Cup in 1973, a year after it was first contested. Originally between the winners of the European Cup and of the European Cup Winners' Cup, and first played over two legs, since 1999, it has matched the Champions League and UEFA Cup winners in a one-off match in Monaco. Here is Liverpool's full UEFA Super Cup record.

1977 1ST LEG
VOLKSPARKSTADION, HAMBURG, 22 NOVEMBER 1977

Hamburg SV (1) **1**   **v**   **Liverpool** (0) **1**

Keller (29)   Fairclough (65)

Att. 16,000

Liverpool: Clemence, Neal, Jones (Smith), Thompson, Hughes,
R. Kennedy, Case (Johnson), Callaghan, Heighway, Dalglish, Fairclough

2ND LEG
ANFIELD, LIVERPOOL, 6 DECEMBER 1977

Liverpool (2) **6**   **v**   **Hamburg SV** (0) **0**

Thompson (21)

McDermott (40, 56, 57)

Fairclough (84)

Dalglish (88)

Liverpool won 7–1 on aggregate

Att. 34,931

Liverpool: Clemence, Neal, Smith, Thompson, Hughes, R. Kennedy, McDermott,
Heighway (Johnson), Case, Dalglish, Fairclough

1978 1ST LEG
PARC ASTRID, BRUSSELS, 4 DECEMBER 1978

Anderlecht (2) **3**   **v**   **Liverpool** (1) **1**

Vercauteren (17)   Case (27)

Vander Elst (38),

Rensenbrink (87)

Att. 35,000

Liverpool: Clemence, Neal, A. Kennedy, Hughes, Hansen, R. Kennedy, Case,
McDermott, Souness, Dalglish, Johnson (Heighway)

2ND LEG

ANFIELD, LIVERPOOL, 19 DECEMBER 1978

Liverpool (1) 2   v   **Anderlecht** (0) **1**

Hughes (13)   Vander Elst (71)

Fairclough (87)

Liverpool lost 4–3 on aggregate

Att. 23,598

Liverpool: Ogrizovic, Neal, Hughes, Thompson, Hansen,
R. Kennedy, Case, McDermott, Souness, Dalglish, Fairclough

1984

STADIO COMMUNALE, TURIN, 16 JANUARY 1985

Juventus (1) **2**   v   **Liverpool (0) 0**

Boniek (39, 79)

Att. 55,384

Liverpool: Grobbelaar, Neal, Kennedy, Lawrenson, Hansen,
Nicol, Whelan, McDonald, Wark, Rush, Walsh

2001

STADE LOUIS II, MONACO, 24 AUGUST 2001

Liverpool (2) **3**   v   Bayern Munich (0) 2

Riise (23), Heskey (45)   Salihamidzic (57)

Owen (46)   Jancker (82)

Att. 15,000

Liverpool: Westerveld, Babbel, Henchoz, Hyypia, Carragher, Gerrard (Biscan),
Hamann, McAllister, Riise (Murphy),
Owen (Fowler), Heskey

2005

STADE LOUIS II, MONACO, 26 AUGUST 2005

Liverpool (0) **3**   v   CSKA Moscow (1) 1

Cisse (82, 103)   Carvalho (28)

Luis Garcia (109)

Att. 16,000

Liverpool: Reina, Finnan (Sinama-Pongolle), Hyypia, Riise (Cisse),
Luis Garcia, Alonso (Sissoko), Hamann, Josemi, Morientes,
Carragher, Zenden

Liverpool club captains

Below is a list of the players who were captain of Liverpool on a regular basis:

Andrew Hannah	1892–1895	Phil Taylor	1950–1953
Jimmy Ross	1895–1897	Bill Jones	1953–1954
John McCartney	1897–1898	Laurie Hughes	1954–1955
Harry Storer	1898–1899	Billy Liddell	1955–1958
Alex Raisbeck	1899–1909	Johnny Wheeler	1958–1959
Arthur Goddard	1909–1912	Ronnie Moran	1959–1960
Ephraim Longworth	1912–1913	Dick White	1960–1961
Harry Lowe	1913–1915	Ron Yeats	1961–1970
Ephraim Longworth/		Tommy Smith	1970–1973
Don MacKinlay	1919–1920	Emlyn Hughes	1973–1979
Ephraim Longworth	1920–1921	Phil Thompson	1979–1982
Don MacKinlay	1921–1928	Graeme Souness	1982–1984
Tom Bromilow	1928–1929	Phil Neal	1984–1985
James Jackson	1929–1930	Alan Hansen	1985–1988
Tom Morrison	1930–1931	Ronnie Whelan	1988–1989
Tom Bradshaw	1931–1934	Alan Hansen	1989–1990
Ernie Blenkinsop/		Ronnie Whelan	1990–1991
Tom Cooper	1934–1935	Steve Nicol	1990–1991
Ernie Blenkinsop	1935–1936	Mark Wright	1991–1993
Ernie Blenkinsop/		Ian Rush	1993–1996
Tom Cooper	1936–1937	John Barnes	1996–1997
Tom Cooper	1937–1939	Paul Ince	1997–1999
Matt Busby	1939–1940	Jamie Redknapp	1999–2002
Willie Fagan	1945–1947	Sami Hyypia	2001–2003
Jack Balmer	1947–1950	Steven Gerrard	2003–

Playing in pain

Phil Neal hated missing training and matches so much that when he broke his foot he had a specially adapted football boot made so that it eased the pain when he was playing.

Derby goal king

When Ian Rush left Liverpool in 1986, he had scored 25 goals against Everton, more than any other player in the history of Merseyside derby matches. This record still stands today.

FA Youth Cup winners

Liverpool's first win in the FA Youth Cup came in 1996 with a team that included Jamie Carragher and Michael Owen. The young Reds beat West Ham United's juniors (containing Frank Lampard and Rio Ferdinand) 4–1 on aggregate in the final. In 2005–06, Liverpool overcame Manchester City 3–2 on aggregate to win the competition for a second time. Twelve months later, under coach Steve Heighway, the Reds became only the fifth team to retain the FA Youth Cup when they won a penalty shoot out against Manchester United at Old Trafford after the final had ended 2–2 on aggregate. The only goal of the second leg came from Robbie Threlfall, who had suffered the misfortune of scoring an own goal in the 2–1 loss at Anfield. In the shoot-out – only the second in FA Youth Cup final history – Liverpool triumphed 4–3.

Reds at the World Cup

Player	Country	Year	Matches	Goals
Alan A'Court	England	1958	3	0
Daniel Agger	Denmark	2010	3	0
Xabi Alonso	Spain	2006	3	1
John Barnes	England	1990	5	0
Peter Beardsley	England	1990	4	0
Stig Inge Bjornebye	Norway	1994	3	0
Ian Callaghan	England	1966	1	0
Jamie Carragher	England	2006/2010	6	0
Peter Crouch	England	2006	4	1
Kenny Dalglish	Scotland	1978/1982	5	2
El Hadji Diouf	Senegal	2002	5	0
Jerzy Dudek	Poland	2002	2	0
Brad Friedel	USA	1998	1	0
Luis Garcia	Spain	2006	3	0
Steven Gerrard	England	2006/2010	9	2
Gary Gillespie	Scotland	1990	1	0
Dietmar Hamann	Germany	2002	6	0
Alan Hansen	Scotland	1982	3	0
Emile Heskey	England	2002	5	1
Ray Houghton	Ireland	1990	5	0
Laurie Hughes	England	1950	3	0
Roger Hunt	England	1966	6	3
Glenn Hysen	Sweden	1990	2	0
Paul Ince	England	1998	4	0
Glenn Johnson	England	2010	4	0
Harry Kewell	Australia	2006	3	1
Dirk Kuyt	Holland	2010	7	1
Sotirios Kyrgiakos	Greece	2010	2	0
Oyvind Leonhardsen	Norway	1998	3	0
Javier Mascherano	Argentina	2010	4	0
Steve McMahon	England	1990	3	0
Steve McManaman	England	1998	1	0
Jan Molby	Denmark	1986	4	0
Phil Neal	England	1982	2	0
Steve Nicol	Scotland	1986	3	0
Michael Owen	England	1998/2002	9	4
Maxi Rodriguez	Argentina	2010	5	0
Martin Skrtel	Slovakia	2010	4	0
Graeme Souness	Scotland	1978/1982	4	1
Steve Staunton	Ireland	1990	5	0
Phil Thompson	England	1982	5	0
Fernando Torres	Spain	2010	7	0
Ronnie Whelan	Ireland	1990	1	0
Abel Xavier	Portugal	2002	1	0
Tommy Younger	Scotland	1958	2	0

European travellers

Liverpool are one of the most travelled of all English clubs. They have played European ties in 40 countries and it would have been 41 if the Reds' Champions League match against Maccabi Haifa had been played in Israel rather than in Kiev, Ukraine. These are the 40 (country names are contemporary, i.e. what they were when Liverpool played the matches).

Austria • Belarus • Belgium • Bulgaria • Cyprus • Czech Republic • Denmark • East Germany • England • Finland • France • Germany • Greece • Holland • Hungary • Iceland • Italy • Lithuania • Luxembourg • Macedonia • Northern Ireland • Norway • Poland • Portugal • Republic of Ireland • Romania • Russia • Scotland • Serbia • Slovakia • Slovenia • Soviet Union • Spain • Sweden • Switzerland • Turkey • Ukraine • Wales • West Germany • Yugoslavia

Shankly receives FIFA honour

In 1999, 18 years after his death, Bill Shankly was awarded a place in the FIFA International Football Hall of Fame.

500 and counting

Yossi Benayoun scored Liverpool's 500th goal in European competitions on 6 November 2007, against Besiktas in the the UEFA Champions League. The Reds went on to rout the Turkish club 8–0, with Benayoun grabbing a hat-trick.

Liverpool managers

1892–1896	**John McKenna/**	1983–1985	**Joe Fagan**
	William Barclay		1 Football League
1896–1915	**Tom Watson**		1 League Cup
	2 Football League		1 European Cup
1920–1923	**David**	1985–1991	**Kenny Dalglish**
	Ashworth		3 Football League
	1 Football League		2 FA Cup
1923–1928	**Matt McQueen**	1991–1994	**Graeme Souness**
	1 League title		1 FA Cup
1928–1936	**George**	1994–1998	**Roy Evans**
	Patterson		League Cup
1936–1951	**George Kay**	1998	**Roy Evans/**
	1 Football League		**Gerard Houllier**
1951–1956	**Don Welsh**	1998–2004	**Gerard Houllier**
1956–1959	**Phil Taylor**		1 UEFA Cup
1959–1974	**Bill Shankly**		1 FA Cup
	3 Football League		1 League Cup
	2 FA Cups	2004–2010	**Rafael Benitez**
	1 UEFA Cup		1 Champions
1974–1983	**Bob Paisley**		League
	6 Football League		1 FA Cup
	3 League Cup	2010–2011	**Roy Hodgson**
	3 European Cup	2011–2012	**Kenny Dalglish**
	1 UEFA Cup		1 League Cup
	1 European	2012–	**Brendan Rodgers**
	Super Cup		

More medals than League games

Goalkeeper Pegguy Arphexad spent three seasons at Liverpool and collected six medals with the Reds, two in the League Cup, and one each in the FA Cup, UEFA Cup, FA Charity Shield and UEFA Super Cup. Strangely, in every case, the Frenchman was an unused substitute. Arphexad's medal count matched the number of appearances he made for Liverpool, two in the Premier League, two in the League Cup and two in the UEFA Champions League. Not only did Liverpool win all six matches in which Arphexad played, but they scored 27 goals and conceded just three in them.

DID YOU KNOW THAT?
Arphexad also won a League Cup winners' medal with Leicester City in 2000 as an unused substitute.

Fortress Anfield

Liverpool is one of only two clubs in the history of the Football League/Premier League to win every home match in a season and in all competitions. They did in 1893–94 – a season in which they were also undefeated on their travels in the League – winning their 14 Division Two contests, plus two ties in the FA Cup and a promotion play-off game (then called Test matches). Brentford emulated the feat in season 1929–30, when they were runners-up in Division Three South, and Sheffield Wednesday's only blemish in 1899–1900 came with a home reverse against neighbours Sheffield United in the FA Cup.

Reds in Europe

Liverpool have won more European trophies than any other English club with five European Cups and three UEFA Cups. This is their season-by-season record in the three main competitions:

Year	Competition	Home						Away				
		P	W	D	L	F	A	W	D	L	F	A
1964–65	**European Cup**	9	3	1	0	12	2	2	2	1	8	5
1965–66	**Cup Winners' Cup**	9	4	0	0	9	1	1	1	3	3	5
1966–67	**European Cup**	5	1	1	0	4	2	1	0	2	4	8
1967–68	**Fairs Cup**	6	2	0	1	10	2	1	0	2	3	3
1968–69	**Fairs Cup**	2	1	0	0	2	1	0	0	1	1	2
1969–70	**Fairs Cup**	4	2	0	0	13	2	1	0	1	2	1
1970–71	**Fairs Cup**	10	4	0	1	9	1	1	4	0	4	3
1971–72	**Cup Winners' Cup**	4	1	1	0	2	0	0	0	2	2	5
1972–73	**UEFA Cup**	12	6	0	0	14	1	2	2	2	5	5
1973–74	**European Cup**	4	1	0	1	3	2	0	1	1	2	3
1974–75	**Cup Winners' Cup**	4	1	1	0	12	1	1	1	0	1	0
1975–76	**UEFA Cup**	12	5	1	0	18	5	3	2	1	7	4
1976–77	**European Cup**	9	4	0	0	11	1	3	0	2	11	4
1977–78	**European Cup**	7	3	0	0	12	2	2	0	2	5	5
1978–79	**European Cup**	2	0	1	0	0	0	0	0	1	0	2
1979–80	**European Cup**	2	1	0	0	2	1	0	0	1	0	3
1980–81	**European Cup**	9	3	0	1	19	2	3	2	0	5	2
1981–82	**European Cup**	6	3	0	0	11	2	1	1	1	3	4
1982–83	**European Cup**	6	3	0	0	9	2	1	0	2	4	4
1983–84	**European Cup**	9	3	1	0	7	0	4	1	0	9	3
1984–85	**European Cup**	9	4	0	0	15	2	2	1	2	3	3
1991–92	**UEFA Cup**	8	3	0	1	14	3	1	0	3	2	5
1992–93	**Cup Winners' Cup**	4	1	0	1	6	3	1	0	1	4	5
1995–96	**UEFA Cup**	4	0	1	1	0	1	1	1	0	2	1

Year	Competition	Home						Away				
		P	W	D	L	F	A	W	D	L	F	A
1996–97	**Cup Winners' Cup**	8	4	0	0	14	4	2	1	1	4	5
1997–98	**UEFA Cup**	4	1	1	0	2	0	0	1	1	2	5
1998–99	**UEFA Cup**	6	1	1	1	5	1	1	1	1	6	5
2000–01	**UEFA Cup**	13	4	1	1	6	1	4	3	0	13	8
2001–02	**Champions League**	16	5	2	1	12	5	1	5	1	11	7
2002–03	**Champions League**	6	1	1	1	6	2	1	1	1	6	6
2002–03	**UEFA Cup**	6	2	0	1	3	2	2	1	0	3	1
2003–04	**UEFA Cup**	8	3	1	0	7	1	1	2	1	7	6
2004–05	**Champions League**	15	5	1	1	11	4	3	3	2	9	6
2005–06	**Champions League**	14	3	2	2	8	3	5	1	1	12	4
2006–07	**Champions League**	15	6	0	1	12	4	3	2	3	10	8
2007–08	**Champions League**	14	5	1	1	23	5	3	2	2	11	7
2008–09	**Champions League**	12	4	1	1	11	5	3	3	0	11	7
2009–10	**Champions League**	6	1	0	2	3	4	1	1	1	2	3
2009–10*	**Europa League**	8	4	0	0	9	2	1	0	3	4	5
2010–11	**Europa League**	7	5	2	0	11	2	2	4	1	5	3
2012–13	**Europa League**	12	3	2	1	12	7	4	0	2	8	6

* Third-placed teams after the Champions League goup stage enter the Europa League.

Derby under lights

The first floodlit match at Anfield was played on 30 October 1957, when Everton provided the opposition in a match to commemorate the 75th anniversary of the Liverpool County FA. Liverpool won the game 3–2, with Billy Liddell scoring twice. Those first Anfield floodlights, which cost £15,000 to install, were mounted on pylons set in each of the ground's four corners. They were removed in 1973 and replaced with two new sets across the roof of the Kemlyn Stand and the Main Stand.

Premier League hat-tricks

Since the FA Premier League began in 1992, 13 Liverpool players have scored League hat-tricks.

Date	Player	Opposition	Venue
17.4.93	**Mark Walters**	Coventry City	Anfield
30.10.93	**Robbie Fowler**	Southampton	Anfield
28.8.94	**Robbie Fowler**	Arsenal	Anfield
23.9.95	**Robbie Fowler (4)**	Bolton Wanderers	Anfield
23.12.95	**Robbie Fowler**	Arsenal	Anfield
14.12.96	**Robbie Fowler (4)**	Middlesbrough	Anfield
5.10.97	**Patrik Berger**	Chelsea	Anfield
14.2.98	**Michael Owen**	Sheffield Wednesday	Hillsborough
30.8.98	**Michael Owen**	Newcastle United	St James' Park
24.10.98	**Michael Owen (4)**	Nottingham Forest	Anfield
21.11.98	**Robbie Fowler**	Aston Villa	Villa Park
16.1.99	**Robbie Fowler**	Southampton	Anfield
6.9.00	**Michael Owen**	Aston Villa	Anfield
15.10.00	**Emile Heskey**	Derby County	Pride Park
5.5.01	**Michael Owen**	Newcastle United	Anfield
20.10.01	**Robbie Fowler**	Leicester City	Filbert Street
28.9.02	**Michael Owen**	Manchester City	Maine Road
26.4.03	**Michael Owen (4)**	WBA	The Hawthorns
13.11.04	**Milan Baros**	Crystal Palace	Anfield
31.3.07	**Peter Crouch**	Arsenal	Anfield
23.2.08	**Fernando Torres**	Middlesbrough	Anfield
15.3.08	**Fernando Torres**	West Ham United	Anfield
22.3.09	**Steven Gerrard**	Aston Villa	Anfield
12.9.09	**Yossi Benayoun**	Burnley	Anfield
26.9.09	**Fernando Torres**	Hull City	Anfield
6.3.11	**Dirk Kuyt**	Manchester United	Anfield
1.5.11	**Maxi Rodriguez**	Birmingham City	Anfield
9.5.11	**Maxi Rodriguez**	Fulham	Craven Cottage
13.3.12	**Steven Gerrard**	Everton	Anfield
28.4.12	**Luis Suarez**	Norwich City	Carrow Road
29.9.12	**Luis Suarez**	Norwich City	Carrow Road

"The meat" defeat the Reds

On 4 November 1992 Spartak Moscow became the only team to beat Liverpool at Anfield in the European Cup Winners' Cup. After winning 4–2 (Wright, McManaman) in Moscow, the Russians won 2–0 in the return. Spartak are nicknamed "The Meat" because they were sponsored by a Moscow-based meat company in the club's early years.

Luck of the Irish

Five of the 10 Republic of Ireland internationals to win a European Cup/UEFA Champions League winners' medal did so with Liverpool: Steve Heighway, Mark Lawrenson, Ronnie Whelan, Michael Robinson and Steve Finnan.

Rafa's men rule Anfield

On 30 October 2002 Rafa Benitez and his Valencia visited Anfield for a UEFA Champions League game. The Spaniards came away with a 1–0 win, having already beaten Liverpool 2–0 in the Mestalla.

DID YOU KNOW KNOW THAT?
Rafael Benitez is the only manager to have won the UEFA Cup and UEFA Champions League in consecutive seasons, and with different clubs. He won the UEFA Cup with Valencia in 2004 and guided Liverpool to UEFA Champions League glory in 2005.

TV stars

A number of Liverpool players have appeared on television shows, including:

Alan Hansen
Sky TV (pundit), *Football Focus* (BBC; studio guest),
Match of the Day (BBC; studio guest),
US Masters Golf (BBC), *A Brush With Fame*

Mark Lawrenson
Football Focus (BBC; studio guest),
Match of the Day (BBC; studio guest)

Phil Thompson
Sky Sports Special (studio guest)

Ronnie Whelan
You're On Sky Sports (studio guest)

Paul Walsh
Sky Sports Special (match reporter and studio guest)

Ian Rush
Sky Sports Special (match reporter)

Jamie Redknapp
Sky Sports Super Sunday/Monday Night Football (studio guest)
A League of Their Own (Sky1; team captain)

Kenny Dalglish
Sky Sports Super Sunday/Monday Night Football (studio guest)

John Barnes
ITV Sport (studio guest), *Channel Five Football* (host)

David James
Beyond the NFL (Sky Sports)

Michael Robinson
El Dia Despues (Spanish TV)

Emlyn Hughes
A Question of Sport (BBC), *Sporting Triangles* (ITV)

John Aldridge
Spanish Football on Sky Sports

Jim Beglin
ITV Sport (match reporter)

Jamie Carragher
A Question of Sport, European Championship coverage (ITV; pundit)

Brendan Rodgers and the Liverpool FC Squad
Being Liverpool (Channel 5)

The voice of Anfield

George Sephton began his public address announcing duties at Anfield in 1971–72 and he celebrated his 42nd season with the club in 2012–13.

Super Phil

Phil Neal is the only English player to score in two European Cup Finals in open play. He scored Liverpool's third against Borussia Moenchengladbach 1977 and gave the Reds the lead against AS Roma in 1984 (he also converted a penalty in the shoot-out, as did Alan Kennedy, the winner in 1981).

When Carra passed Cally

When Jamie Carragher played in the UEFA Champions League semi-final second leg against Chelsea in 2007, it was his 90th game in European competition for Liverpool. It took him past Ian Callaghan's previous record of 89 European matches between 1964 and 1978. Stephen Gerrard became the second Liverpool player to reach the 100 games plateau against Real Madrid in March 2009.

DID YOU KNOW THAT?
Jamie Carragher is the only Liverpool player to play under six permanent managers: Roy Evans, Gerard Houllier, Rafael Benitez, Roy Hodgson, Kenny Dalglish and Brendan Rodgers.

Liverpool chartbusters

In keeping with the splendid musical heritage of their Merseyside home, Liverpool FC have made several notable forays into the UK's pop music charts. These are the songs that got the Kop rocking:

Date	Track *(Label and Catalogue No.)*	pos	wks
28 May 77	**We Can Do It** (EP) *State STAT 50*	**15**	4
23 Apr 83	**Liverpool** (We're Never Gonna…)/		
	Liverpool Anthem *Mean MEAN 102*	**54**	4
17 May 86	**Sitting on Top of the World**		
	Columbia DB 9116	**50**	2
14 May 88	**Anfield Rap** (Red Machine in Full Effect)		
	Virgin LFC 1	**3**	6
18 May 96	**Pass and Move** (It's the Liverpool Groove)		
	Telstar LFCCD 96 [1]	**4**	5

[1] Liverpool FC and The Boot Room Boyz

© *Courtesy of* The Book of UK Hit Singles & Albums, *published by Guinness World Records and the UK Charts Company.*

Reds are double trouble for United

On 14 March 2009, Liverpool went to Old Trafford and returned home having completed a Premier League double over the defending Premier League champions Manchester United. Fernando Torres, Steven Gerrard, Fabio Aurelio and Andrea Dossena scored in the 4–1 victory. Six months earlier, at Anfield Liverpool had won 2–1 courtesy of a Wes Brown own goal and the winner from Ryan Babel.

Britain's most expensive teenager

Ian Rush became Britain's then most expensive teenager when Bob Paisley paid Chester £300,000 for his services in March 1980.

Pope supports Liverpool

In 2004 Pope John Paul II met players from the Polish national football team. During their visit to the Vatican, the pontiff informed Liverpool goalkeeper Jerzy Dudek that he was a keen supporter of Liverpool and listened out for their results whenever they were playing.

Alonso's long-distance double

On Saturday 7 January 2006 Liverpool met Championship club Luton Town in the FA Cup third round at Kenilworth Road. By the hour mark, the Reds were 3–1 down and facing an early Cup exit. However, they staged a remarkable comeback to win 5–3, the pick of the goals coming from Xabi Alonso, who scored with a 30-yard effort to equalise at 3–3. Then, with his side trailing 4–3, Luton goalkeeper Marlon Beresford went forward for a stoppage-time corner. The ball broke to Alonso who ignored calls from skipper Steven Gerrard for a pass, and fired the ball from 12 yards inside his own half into the back of the Hatters' net. Gerrard and Florent Sinama-Pongolle (2) scored the Reds' other goals.

A second home

It is no wonder that Liverpool considered Wembley to be their second home. In the 41 years from 1971 to 2012, the Reds played there 32 times and their record at "the Venue of Legends" was P32, W16, D7, L9.

Year	Competition	Opponents	Result	Score
2012	**FA Cup final**	Chelsea	L	1–2
2012	**FA Cup semi-final**	Everton	W	2–1
2012	**Carling Cup final**	Cardiff City	D	2–2**
1996	**FA Cup Final**	Manchester United	L	0–1
1995	**League Cup Final**	Bolton Wanderers	W	2–1
1992	**FA Charity Shield**	Leeds United	L	3–4
1992	**FA Cup Final**	Sunderland	W	2–0
1990	**FA Charity Shield**	Manchester United	D	1–1*
1989	**FA Charity Shield**	Arsenal	W	1–0
1989	**FA Cup Final**	Everton	W	3–2*
1988	**FA Charity Shield**	Wimbledon	W	2–1
1988	**FA Cup Final**	Wimbledon	L	0–1
1987	**League Cup Final**	Arsenal	L	1–2*
1986	**FA Charity Shield**	Everton	D	1–1*
1986	**FA Cup Final**	Everton	W	3–1
1984	**FA Charity Shield**	Everton	L	0–1
1984	**League Cup Final**	Everton	D	0–0*
1983	**FA Charity Shield**	Manchester United	L	0–2
1983	**League Cup Final**	Manchester United	W	2–1*
1982	**FA Charity Shield**	Tottenham Hotspur	W	1–0
1982	**League Cup Final**	Tottenham Hotspur	W	3–1*
1981	**League Cup Final**	West Ham United	D	1–1*
1980	**FA Charity Shield**	West Ham United	W	1–0
1979	**FA Charity Shield**	Arsenal	W	3–1
1978	**European Cup Final**	FC Bruges	W	1–0
1978	**League Cup Final**	Nottingham Forest	D	0–0*
1977	**FA Charity Shield**	Manchester United	D	0–0*
1977	**FA Cup Final**	Manchester United	L	1–2
1976	**FA Charity Shield**	Southampton	W	1–0
1974	**FA Charity Shield**	Leeds United	D/W	1–1**
1974	**FA Cup Final**	Newcastle United	W	3–0
1971	**FA Cup Final**	Arsenal	L	1–2*

* = After extra time; ** = Won on penalties after extra time.

Last of the long ties

On 27 February 1991 Liverpool and Everton played in the last ever second replay in an FA Cup tie. Everton won the fifth-round match 1–0.

Don't I recognise you from somewhere?

In April 2009, Liverpool played Chelsea in the quarter-final of UEFA Champions League. Amazingly, this was the fifth consecutive season in which the two English powerhouses had met. Liverpool won two semi-finals, 1–0 on aggregate in 2004–05 and 4–1 on penalties in 2006–07 (the aggregate score was 1–1); Chelsea won the 2007–08 semi-final 4–3 on aggregate and this 2008–09 quarter-final 7–5 on aggregate; and, in 2005–06, the teams played out a pair of goalless draws in the group stage.

Stevie G completes goal century

On 1 October 2008, Liverpool captain Steven Gerrard scored his 100th goal for the club in a 3–1 Champions League victory over PSV Eindhoven at Anfield. Playing mainly as an attacking midfielder, he has an outstanding goalscoring record, averaging better than a goal every four matches. Gerrard moved into the top ten of the Liverpool scoring charts early in 2010, and in August 2012 he netted

Most-capped England internationals

Liverpool have had 59 players capped by England. Here are the 17 who made at least 20 appearances for England whilst Liverpool players (up to 1 June 2013):

Player	Caps	Goals	Player	Caps	Goals
Steven Gerrard	102	19	Roger Hunt	34	18
Michael Owen	60	26	Peter Beardsley	34	6
Emlyn Hughes	59	1	Glen Johnson	33	0
Ray Clemence	56	0	Kevin Keegan	29	7
Phil Neal	50	5	Peter Crouch	28	14
John Barnes	48	8	Terry McDermott	25	3
Phil Thompson	42	1	Steve McManaman	24	0
Jamie Carragher	38	0	Robbie Fowler	22	5
Emile Heskey	35	5			

Liverpool's sunshine boy

Anfield, Liverpool fans used to sing a song in honour of Luis Garcia, based on the tune of "You Are My Sunshine".

Eight As for the Reds

As at May 2013, eight Liverpool players whose surname ended with the letter "A" had scored Premier League goals for the Reds: Nicolas Anelka, Alvaro Arbeloa, Titi Camara, Andrea Dossena, Luis Garcia, Sami Hyypia, Lucas Leiva and Albert Reira. Emiliano Insua and Gabriel Paletta scored in the League Cup.

Champions League Turkish delight

On 6 November 2007, Liverpool set a new UEFA Champions League record when they crushed Besiktas 8–0 at Anfield. The two teams had met in Turkey two weeks earlier and the Reds had lost 2–1. They made no mistake in the return. Yossi Benayoun led the way with a hat-trick, while Peter Crouch and Ryan Babel both scored twice and Steven Gerrard once. The 8–0 score is a UEFA Champions League record; the European Cup mark was set in 1973–74, when Dinamo Bucharest beat Crusaders of Northern Ireland, 11–0. Liverpool's biggest win in Europe is also 11–0, in the 1974–75 European Cup-Winners' Cup. Stromsgodset of Norway were seen off, with Phil Boersma (2), Phil Thompson (2), Phil Neal, Tommy Smith, Alec Linday, Peter Cormack, Emlyn Hughes, Steve Heighway, Ray Kennedy and Ian Callaghan scoring.

Gerrard makes it to 500

On 5 December 2009 Liverpool captain Steven Gerrard played his 500th game for the Reds in a goalless Premier League draw against Blackburn Rovers at Ewood Park.

Fastest Premiership hat-trick

Robbie Fowler scored three goals in 4 minutes and 33 seconds against Arsenal at Anfield on 28 August 1994. The fastest ever Premier League hat-trick gave the Reds a 3–0 win.

Liverpool's 1,000th Premier League goal

On 13 September 2008, Manchester United's Wes Brown scored an own goal for Liverpool's equaliser at Anfield. It was the Reds' 1,000th goal in the Premier League since it began in 1992. Liverpool went on to win the game 2–1.

Hicks and Gillett

In February 2007, Liverpool FC was bought by American businessmen George Gillett and Thomas Hicks. Both men had experience of owning sports teams in North America: Gillett controlled the National Hockey League's Montreal Canadiens, while Hicks was the managing general partner of the NHL's Dallas Stars and baseball's Texas Rangers.

They must be doing something right

Although Liverpool secured no silverware in the 2009–10 season, 12 Reds players made it into their countries' FIFA World Cup 2010 finals squads, seven more than Manchester United. They were: Steven Gerrard, Glen Johnson, Jamie Carragher (England); Javier Mascherano, Maxi Rodriguez (Argentina); Dirk Kuyt, Ryan Babel (Holland); Fernando Torres, Pepe Reina (Spain); Daniel Agger (Denmark); Soritios Kyrgiakos (Greece); and Martin Skrtel (Slovakia).

Kings of Europe

Liverpool are easily the most successful British club in European football. They have played and won more matches than any other club. The top four British teams' records are:

Team	Played	Won	Drawn	Lost	GF	GA
Liverpool	344	191	76	77	605	283
Manchester U	317	163	83	67	570	251
Rangers	299	125	78	104	483	395
Celtic	252	123	41	88	300	256

New dawn at Anfield

On 15 October 2010, Tom Hicks and George Gillett sold Liverpool Football Club to New England Sports Ventures, fronted by John W Henry and Tom Werner. NESV owns the famous Boston Red Sox baseball team which won its first championship for 86 years in 2004. Both men had previously invested in other baseball teams: Henry in the New York Yankees and Florida Marlins and Werner in the San Diego Padres.

Record deal

On 31 January 2011, Liverpool received their record transfer fee when Chelsea paid the Reds a British club to British club record £50 million for striker Fernanado Torres.

Life's a beach

One of the strangest ever Premier League goals was scored against Liverpool at the Stadium of Light on 17 October 2009. The Reds lost 1–0 to Sunderland when Darren Bent's shot struck a beach ball which had bounced onto the pitch and wrong-footed Pepe Reina. The ball auctioned in aid of Alder Hey Children's Hospital in Liverpool and was won by Sunderland fan Kevin Barlow, but it is now on display at the National Football Museum in Preston.

Approaching the half-century

Season 2011–12 was the 49th consecutive enjoyed in the top flight by Liverpool. Only Arsenal (92 years) and Everton (57), of the current top division, have longer unbroken runs.

The return of King Kenny

On 8 January 2011, Liverpool announced that manager Roy Hodgson had left the club by mutual consent and that former Anfield legend, Kenny Dalglish, had been appointed as his replacement. The Reds were 12th in the Premier League table at the time. However, despite the team's much-improved performances, they only finished sixth in the Premier League and failed to qualify for European competition for the first time in 12 years. Although he guided Liverpool to League Cup success in 2012, Kenny left the club in May 2012.

Hey, big spenders

During the 2010–11 season, Liverpool broke their transfer record for monies spent on a player. On 31 January 2011, the Reds paid a club record fee of £35 million for Andy Carroll from Newcastle United.

120 years at Anfield

The 2011–12 season was Liverpool's 120th season as a club and their 120th at Anfield.

Liverbirds slay Bluebirds

After seeing off Exeter City, Brighton and Hove Albion, Stoke City, Chelsea and Manchester City in the earlier rounds, Liverpool went on to beat Cardiff City in the final to win the League Cup in 2011–12 to become the most successful team in the competition's history, with eight wins. The final was played at Wembley Stadium and finished 1–1 after 90 minutes. The Welsh club took the lead in the 18th minute through Joe Mason before Martin Skrtel scored the equalizer in the 60th minute. The game then went into extra-time, with Dirk Kuyt putting Liverpool 2–1 up in the 108th minute, only for Cardiff's Ben Turner to find the net in dramatic fashion in the 118th minute. With the scores level at the end of extra-time, a penalty shootout then followed, which Liverpool won 3–2 to end the club's six-year trophy drought.

Stevie G racks up 400

Steven Gerrard made his 400th league appearance for Liverpool in the Merseyside derby at Anfield on 13 March 2012. The Liverpool captain marked the occasion in style, netting a hat-trick in a comfortable 3–0 victory.

Second Wembley visit

Having not appeared in a Wembley final since 1996, Liverpool appeared in both domestic finals in 2012. After winning the League Cup against Cardiff, they then made it through to the FA Cup final against Chelsea. But it turned out to be a day of disappointment for Liverpool fans: although they produced a battling performance, the Reds lost 2–1 to Chelsea.

Back among the goals

Liverpool scored 71 goals in the 2012–13 Premier League season – an impressive 23 up on their tally from the previous campaign.

Sharing the goalscoring load

Liverpool had 15 Premier League goalscorers in 2012–13 – matching the club's Premier League record, the same number having scored in the 2006–07 and 2008–09 seasons.

When Irish eyes are smiling

On 1 June 2012, Liverpool unveiled Brendan Rodgers as their new manager. Rodgers had guided Swansea City to an impressive 11th place the previous season, their first in the Premier League. His appointment saw him become only the third Irish manager in the club's 120-year history, after John McKenna (1892–96) and David Ashworth (1919–23).

Youngest ever Red

On 26 September 2012, Jerome Sinclair became the youngest-ever player to appear in a competitive match for Liverpool: he was 16 years 6 days old when he played during the Reds' 2–1 away victory over West Bromwich Albion in the third round of the League Cup.

The boy from Brazil

Philippe Coutinho was once hailed as "the future of Inter" by no less an observer than former Liverpool manager Rafa Benitez. He joined the club for £8.5 million in January 2013 and already it appears to have been a shrewd piece of business. Showing pace, trickery, vision and an enviable eye for goal, the 20-year-old seems set to remain an integral part of the Liverpool set-up for many years to come.

CHAPTER 2

WE ARE THE CHAMPIONS

The heading says it all. "We are the champions." And the best of all is that, as a Liverpool fan, you and your predecessors have been able to make that boast on 18 occasions. Only those other Reds, from along the East Lancs Road, can make that claim.

Liverpool's run of success in the twentieth century in Division One of the Football League Championship was truly astonishing. In the 90 years of competition, there were 10 seasons, during the two World Wars, when it was not contested, Liverpool FC won the title on average once every five seasons. Some of these titles were won at a canter, with everyone trailing in the Reds' mighty wake; other were more closely run affairs with the destination of the silverware not known until the final day of the season.

Over the next 18 pages, you can relive every one of these Football League Championship winning campaigns, with notable moments and key fixtures, combined with the final table, so you can see just how the title was won and lost.

Liverpool FC has had more great managers, fantastic players and incredible stories than perhaps any rival in Europe. Relive them here, and then think about what the future will bring to Anfield and the Kop.

1900–01

Liverpool won the first of their 18 First Division Championships in 1900–01. Sunderland pressed Liverpool hard all season and beat the Reds 2–1 (Charlie Wilson) at Anfield on 29 September 1900 in the fifth game of the League campaign. On 16 February 1901 Liverpool lost 1–0 away to Bolton Wanderers in a game that was originally scheduled for 2 February 1901, but was rearranged following the death of Queen Victoria on 22 January. In their next game Liverpool faced Sunderland at Roker Park in a game that was to mark the turning point of the season. Liverpool won 1–0 (Jack Cox) on 23 February, then went on to win eight and draw three of their remaining eleven League games to clinch their maiden First Division Championship by two points from the Rokerites.

		P	W	D	L	F	A	W	D	L	F	A	Pts
1.	**Liverpool FC**	34	12	2	3	36	13	7	5	5	23	22	45
2.	Sunderland	34	12	3	2	43	11	3	10	4	14	15	43
3.	Notts County	34	13	2	2	39	18	5	2	10	15	28	40
4.	Nottingham Forest	34	10	4	3	32	14	6	3	8	21	22	39
5.	Bury	34	11	3	3	31	10	5	4	8	22	27	39
6.	Newcastle United	34	10	5	2	27	13	4	5	8	15	24	38
7.	Everton	34	10	4	3	37	17	6	1	10	18	25	37
8.	Sheffield Wednesday	34	13	2	2	38	16	0	8	9	14	26	36
9.	Blackburn Rovers	34	9	4	4	24	18	3	5	9	15	29	33
10.	Bolton Wanderers	34	10	5	2	21	12	3	2	12	18	43	33
11.	Manchester City	34	12	3	2	32	16	1	3	13	16	42	32
12.	Derby County	34	10	4	3	43	18	2	3	12	12	24	31
13.	Wolverhampton W.	34	6	10	1	21	15	3	3	11	18	40	31
14.	Sheffield United	34	8	4	5	22	23	4	3	10	13	29	31
15.	Aston Villa	34	8	5	4	32	18	2	5	10	13	33	30
16.	Stoke City	34	8	3	6	23	15	3	2	12	23	42	27
17.	Preston North End	34	6	4	7	29	30	3	3	11	20	45	25
18.	West Bromwich Albion	34	4	4	9	21	27	3	4	10	14	35	22

1905-06

Following their Division Two success in 1904-05, Liverpool were crowned Division One champions in 1905-06 for the second time in the club's history. Preston North End pushed the Reds hard all season, but a 2-1 (Tom Chorlton, Joe Hewitt) win over their nearest rivals at Deepdale on 24 March 1906 edged the Reds' noses in front and they held on to win three, draw two and lose only one of their remaining six League games to clinch the Division One Championship title by four points. Liverpool's away form was erratic – they won nine and lost eight of their 17 games on the road, including a 1-3 (Robbie Robinson) defeat on the opening day of the season to Woolwich Arsenal. They also enjoyed a 5-1 (Hewitt 3, John Carlin 2) win away at Middlesbrough.

		P	W	D	L	F	A	W	D	L	F	A	Pts
1.	**Liverpool FC**	38	14	3	2	49	15	9	2	8	30	31	51
2.	Preston North End	38	12	5	2	36	15	5	8	6	18	24	47
3.	Sheffield Wednesday	38	12	5	2	40	20	6	3	10	23	32	44
4.	Newcastle United	38	12	4	3	49	23	6	3	10	25	25	43
5.	Manchester City	38	11	2	6	46	23	8	3	8	27	31	43
6.	Bolton Wanderers	38	13	1	5	51	22	4	6	9	30	45	41
7.	Birmingham	38	14	2	3	49	20	3	5	11	16	39	41
8.	Aston Villa	38	13	2	4	51	19	4	4	11	21	37	40
9.	Blackburn Rovers	38	10	5	4	34	18	6	3	10	20	34	40
10.	Stoke City	38	12	5	2	41	15	4	2	13	13	40	39
11.	Everton	38	12	1	6	44	30	3	6	10	26	36	37
12.	Woolwich Arsenal	38	12	4	3	43	21	3	3	13	19	43	37
13.	Sheffield United	38	10	4	5	33	23	5	2	12	24	39	36
14.	Sunderland	38	13	2	4	40	21	2	3	14	21	49	35
15.	Derby County	38	10	5	4	27	16	4	2	13	12	42	35
16.	Notts County	38	8	9	2	34	21	3	3	13	21	50	34
17.	Bury	38	8	5	6	30	26	3	5	11	27	48	32
18.	Middlesbrough	38	10	4	5	41	23	0	7	12	15	48	31
19.	Nottingham Forest	38	11	2	6	40	27	2	3	14	18	52	31
20.	Wolverhampton W.	38	7	5	7	38	28	1	2	16	20	71	23

1921-22

Liverpool's first title in 16 years was celebrated in the club"s 30th anniversary season. Tottenham Hotspur were the Reds' closest challengers in the title race, and it was their away form which proved the difference: they collected five more points than Spurs. The Reds dropped only one point against their London rivals, winning 1-0 (Harry Beadles) away on 22 October 1921 and drawing 1-1 (Harry Lewis) at Anfield a week later. In the end, Liverpool, who had finished fourth in Division One in both of the two previous seasons, had six points in hand over Tottenham, with Burnley another two points behind in third place.

		P	W	D	L	F	A	W	D	L	F	A	Pts
1.	**Liverpool FC**	42	15	4	2	43	15	7	9	5	20	21	57
2.	Tottenham Hotspur	42	15	3	3	43	17	6	6	9	22	22	51
3.	Burnley	42	16	3	2	49	18	6	2	13	23	36	49
4.	Cardiff City	42	13	2	6	40	26	6	8	7	21	27	48
5.	Aston Villa	42	16	3	2	50	19	6	0	15	24	36	47
6.	Bolton Wanderers	42	12	4	5	40	24	8	3	10	28	35	47
7.	Newcastle United	42	11	5	5	36	19	7	5	9	23	26	46
8.	Middlesbrough	42	12	6	3	46	19	4	8	9	33	50	46
9.	Chelsea	42	9	6	6	17	16	8	6	7	23	27	46
10.	Manchester City	42	13	7	1	44	21	5	2	14	21	49	45
11.	Sheffield United	42	11	3	7	32	17	4	7	10	27	37	40
12.	Sunderland	42	13	4	4	46	23	3	4	14	14	39	40
13.	West Bromwich Albion	42	8	6	7	26	23	7	4	10	25	40	40
14.	Huddersfield Town	42	12	3	6	33	14	3	6	12	20	40	39
15.	Blackburn Rovers	42	7	6	8	35	31	6	6	9	19	26	38
16.	Preston North End	42	12	7	2	33	20	1	5	15	9	45	38
17.	Arsenal	42	10	6	5	27	19	5	1	15	20	37	37
18.	Birmingham City	42	9	2	10	25	29	6	5	10	23	31	37
19.	Oldham Athletic	42	8	7	6	21	15	5	4	12	17	35	37
20.	Everton	42	10	7	4	42	22	2	5	14	15	33	36
21.	Bradford City	42	8	5	8	28	30	3	5	13	20	42	32
22.	Manchester United	42	7	7	7	25	26	1	5	15	16	47	28

1922–23

In 1922–23 Liverpool won their second consecutive Football League Championship, their fourth overall. Sunderland – just as they had been in 1900–01 – were Liverpool's closest challengers for the title. The teams met in the second and third games of the season with the Rokerites winning 1–0 at home, but Liverpool gained quick revenge with a 5–1 (Dick Forshaw, Harry Chambers, 2, Dick Johnson, Donald MacKinlay) victory at Anfield, the same score by which they beat Everton at Anfield (Chambers 3, Jock McNab, Tom Bromilow). And, just as in 1922, Liverpool's title-winning margin was six points, having won 26 of their 42 games.

		P	W	D	L	F	A	W	D	L	F	A	Pts
1.	**Liverpool FC**	42	17	3	1	50	13	9	5	7	20	18	60
2.	Sunderland	42	15	5	1	50	25	7	5	9	22	29	54
3.	Huddersfield Town	42	14	2	5	35	15	7	9	5	25	17	53
4.	Newcastle United	42	13	6	2	31	11	5	6	10	14	26	48
5.	Everton	42	14	4	3	41	20	6	3	12	22	39	47
6.	Aston Villa	42	15	3	3	42	11	3	7	11	22	40	46
7.	West Bromwich Albion	42	12	7	2	38	10	5	4	12	20	39	45
8.	Manchester City	42	14	6	1	38	16	3	5	13	12	33	45
9.	Cardiff City	42	15	2	4	51	18	3	5	13	22	41	43
10.	Sheffield United	42	11	7	3	41	20	5	3	13	27	44	42
11.	Arsenal	42	13	4	4	38	16	3	6	12	23	46	42
12.	Tottenham Hotspur	42	11	3	7	34	22	6	4	11	16	28	41
13.	Bolton Wanderers	42	11	8	2	36	17	3	4	14	14	41	40
14.	Blackburn Rovers	42	12	7	2	32	19	2	5	14	15	43	40
15.	Burnley	42	12	3	6	39	24	4	3	14	19	35	38
16.	Preston North End	42	12	3	6	41	26	1	8	12	19	38	37
17.	Birmingham	42	10	4	7	25	19	3	7	11	16	38	37
18.	Middlesbrough	42	11	4	6	41	25	2	6	13	16	38	36
19.	Chelsea	42	5	13	3	29	20	4	5	12	16	33	36
20.	Nottingham Forest	42	12	2	7	25	23	1	6	14	16	47	34
21.	Stoke City	42	7	9	5	28	19	3	1	17	19	48	30
22.	Oldham Athletic	42	9	6	6	21	20	1	4	16	14	45	30

1946–47

Liverpool won their fifth Division One title in 1946–47, by one point over Manchester United. United won the first meeting 5–0 at Maine Road – their home while bomb-damaged Old Trafford was repaired – but when they visited Anfield for what was effectively a Championship decider, and Liverpool's last home game, it was Anfielders who triumphed, 1–0, thanks to a goal from Albert Stubbins. Liverpool then won three and drew one of their final four away games. Some felt their success was helped by their Chairman, Willam McConnell, who had acted as a Government adviser on nutrition during the war. "Billy Mac" ensured the players ate the right foods prior to games.

		P	W	D	L	F	A	W	D	L	F	A	Pts
1.	**Liverpool FC**	42	13	3	5	42	24	12	4	5	42	28	57
2.	Manchester United	42	17	3	1	61	19	5	9	7	34	35	56
3.	Wolverhampton W.	42	15	1	5	66	31	10	5	6	32	25	56
4.	Stoke City	42	14	5	2	52	21	10	2	9	38	32	55
5.	Blackpool	42	14	1	6	38	32	8	5	8	33	38	50
6.	Sheffield United	42	12	4	5	51	32	9	3	9	38	43	49
7.	Preston North End	42	10	7	4	45	27	8	4	9	31	47	47
8.	Aston Villa	42	9	6	6	39	24	9	3	9	28	29	45
9.	Sunderland	42	11	3	7	33	27	7	5	9	32	39	44
10.	Everton	42	13	5	3	40	24	4	4	13	22	43	43
11.	Middlesbrough	42	11	3	7	46	32	6	5	10	27	36	42
12.	Portsmouth	42	11	3	7	42	27	5	6	10	24	33	41
13.	Arsenal	42	9	5	7	43	33	7	4	10	29	37	41
14.	Derby County	42	13	2	6	44	28	5	3	13	29	51	41
15.	Chelsea	42	9	3	9	33	39	7	4	10	36	45	39
16.	Grimsby Town	42	9	6	6	37	35	4	6	11	24	47	38
17.	Blackburn Rovers	42	6	5	10	23	27	8	3	10	22	26	36
18.	Bolton Wanderers	42	8	5	8	30	28	5	3	13	27	41	34
19.	Charlton Athletic	42	6	6	9	34	32	5	6	10	23	39	34
20.	Huddersfield Town	42	11	4	6	34	24	2	3	16	19	55	33
21.	Brentford	42	5	5	11	19	35	4	2	15	26	53	25
22.	Leeds United	42	6	5	10	30	30	0	1	20	15	60	18

1963–64

Liverpool returned to Division One in 1961–62 and, two seasons later, under the masterful guidance of Bill Shankly, won their sixth Division One Championship – the first of his three titles. The men from Anfield finished four points ahead of the defending champions Manchester United but, uncharacteristically, their home form was quite erratic, with five losses in 21 matches. The crunch game came on 4 April with United's visit to Anfield. A 3–0 (Ian Callaghan, Alf Arrowsmith 2) Liverpool win gave them the two points, and although they picked up only one point from their final three League games, the Reds held on for the title.

		P	W	D	L	F	A	W	D	L	F	A	Pts
1.	**Liverpool FC**	42	16	0	5	60	18	10	5	6	32	27	57
2.	Manchester United	42	15	3	3	54	19	8	4	9	36	43	53
3.	Everton	42	14	4	3	53	26	7	6	8	31	38	52
4.	Spurs	42	13	3	5	54	31	9	4	8	43	50	51
5.	Chelsea	42	12	3	6	36	24	8	7	6	36	32	50
6.	Sheffield Wednesday	42	15	3	3	50	24	4	8	9	34	43	49
7.	Blackburn Rovers	42	10	4	7	44	28	8	6	7	45	37	46
8.	Arsenal	42	10	7	4	56	37	4	10	34	45	45
9.	Burnley	42	14	3	4	46	23	3	7	11	25	41	44
10.	West Bromwich Albion	42	9	6	6	43	35	7	5	9	27	26	43
11.	Leicester City	42	9	4	8	33	27	7	7	7	28	31	43
12.	Sheffield United	42	10	6	5	35	22	6	5	10	26	42	43
13.	Nottingham Forest	42	9	5	7	34	24	7	4	10	30	44	41
14.	West Ham United	42	8	7	6	45	38	6	5	10	24	36	40
15.	Fulham	42	11	8	2	45	23	2	5	14	13	42	39
16.	Wolverhampton W.	42	6	9	6	36	34	6	6	9	34	46	39
17.	Stoke City	42	9	6	6	49	33	5	4	12	28	45	38
18.	Blackpool	42	8	6	7	26	29	5	3	13	26	44	35
19.	Aston Villa	42	8	6	7	35	29	3	6	12	27	42	34
20.	Birmingham City	42	7	7	7	33	32	4	0	17	21	60	29
21.	Bolton Wanderers	42	6	5	10	30	35	4	3	14	18	45	28
22.	Ipswich Town	42	9	3	9	38	45	0	4	17	18	76	25

1965–66

The two teams which had contested the 1965 FA Cup final at Wembley battled it out for the 1965–66 Football League title and, again, it was Liverpool who prevailed. A quirk of the fixture schedule meant that Liverpool and Leeds met on consecutive days, 27 and 28 December 1965. In the first encounter, at Anfield, the Reds surprisingly lost 1–0. However, they hit back to win 1–0 at Elland Road (Gordon Milne).

DID YOU KNOW THAT?
Three Liverpool players were in the England 1966 World Cup squad: Roger Hunt, Gerry Byrne and Ian Callaghan.

		P	W	D	L	F	A	W	D	L	F	A	Pts
1	**Liverpool FC**	42	17	2	2	52	15	9	7	5	27	19	61
2	Leeds United	42	14	4	3	49	15	9	5	7	30	23	55
3	Burnley	42	15	3	3	45	20	9	4	8	34	27	55
4	Manchester United	42	12	8	1	50	20	6	7	8	34	39	51
5	Chelsea	42	11	4	6	30	21	11	3	7	35	32	51
6	West Bromwich Albion	42	11	6	4	58	34	8	6	7	33	35	50
7	Leicester City	42	12	4	5	40	28	9	3	9	40	37	49
8	Tottenham Hotspur	42	11	6	4	55	37	5	6	10	20	29	44
9	Sheffield United	42	11	6	4	37	25	5	5	11	19	34	43
10	Stoke City	42	12	6	3	42	22	3	6	12	23	42	42
11	Everton	42	12	6	3	39	1	3	5	13	17	43	41
12	West Ham United	42	12	5	4	46	33	3	4	14	24	50	39
13	Blackpool	42	9	5	7	36	29	5	4	12	19	36	37
14	Arsenal	42	8	8	5	36	31	4	5	12	26	44	37
15	Newcastle United	42	10	5	6	26	20	4	4	13	24	43	37
16	Aston Villa	42	10	3	8	39	34	5	3	13	30	46	36
17	Sheffield Wednesday	42	11	6	4	35	18	3	2	16	21	48	36
18	Nottingham Forest	42	11	3	7	31	26	3	5	13	25	46	36
19	Sunderland	42	13	2	6	36	28	1	6	14	15	44	36
20	Fulham	42	9	4	8	34	37	5	3	13	33	48	35
21	Northampton Town	42	8	6	7	31	32	2	7	12	24	60	33
22	Blackburn Rovers	42	6	1	14	30	36	2	3	16	27	52	20

1972-73

In 1972-73 Liverpool won their eighth Division One title. They began the campaign in red-hot form, beating Manchester City 2-0 (Brian Hall, Ian Callaghan) on the first day of the season at Anfield, and followed that up with a 2-0 win over Manchester United, also at Anfield (John Toshack, Steve Heighway). Arsenal and Leeds United led the chasing pack and the crunch came in Liverpool's penultimate match of the season, when Leeds visited Anfield on Easter Monday. Goals from Peter Cormack and Kevin Keegan sealed a 2-0 Liverpool win and they clinched the Championship by three points from Arsenal, with Leeds a further four adrift.

		P	W	D	L	F	A	W	D	L	F	A	Pts
1.	**Liverpool FC**	42	17	3	1	45	19	8	7	6	27	23	60
2.	Arsenal	42	14	5	2	31	14	9	6	6	26	29	57
3.	Leeds United	42	15	4	2	45	13	6	7	8	26	32	53
4.	Ipswich Town	42	10	7	4	34	20	7	7	7	21	25	48
5.	Wolverhampton W.	42	13	3	5	43	23	5	8	8	23	31	47
6.	West Ham United	42	12	5	4	45	25	5	7	9	22	28	46
7.	Derby County	42	15	3	3	43	18	4	5	12	13	36	46
8.	Tottenham Hotspur	42	10	5	6	33	23	6	8	7	25	25	45
9.	Newcastle United	42	12	6	3	35	19	4	7	10	25	32	45
10.	Birmingham City	42	11	7	3	39	22	4	5	12	14	32	42
11.	Manchester City	42	12	4	5	36	20	3	7	11	21	40	41
12.	Chelsea	42	9	6	6	30	22	4	8	9	19	29	40
13.	Southampton	42	8	11	2	26	17	3	7	11	21	35	40
14.	Sheffield United	42	11	4	6	28	18	4	6	11	23	41	40
15.	Stoke City	42	11	8	2	38	17	3	2	16	23	39	38
16.	Leicester City	42	7	9	5	23	18	3	8	10	17	28	37
17.	Everton	42	9	5	7	27	21	4	6	11	14	28	37
18.	Manchester United	42	9	7	5	24	19	3	6	12	20	41	37
19.	Coventry City	42	9	5	7	27	24	4	4	13	13	31	35
20.	Norwich City	42	7	9	5	22	19	4	1	16	14	44	32
21.	Crystal Palace	42	7	7	7	25	21	2	5	14	16	37	30
22.	West Bromwich Albion	42	8	7	6	25	24	1	3	17	13	38	28

1975-76

In his second season in charge, Bob Paisley guided Liverpool to their record ninth Football League Championship. Their biggest rivals were Queens Park Rangers who, on the opening day of the season, made their intentions known to everyone by beating Liverpool 2–0 at Loftus Road. The Reds only claimed top spot in the League with a 2–0 (John Toshack, Phil Neal) defeat of QPR in the return game at Anfield on 20 December. QPR won more matches during the campaign, 24 to the Reds' 23, but Liverpool's 3–1 (Kevin Keegan, John Toshack, Ray Kennedy) win at Wolverhampton Wanderers in the final game gave them the title by a point.

		P	W	D	L	F	A	W	D	L	F	A	Pts
1.	**Liverpool FC**	42	14	5	2	41	21	9	9	3	25	10	60
2.	Queens Park Rangers	42	17	4	0	42	13	7	7	7	25	20	59
3.	Manchester United	42	16	4	1	40	13	7	6	8	28	29	56
4.	Derby County	42	15	3	3	45	30	6	8	7	30	28	53
5.	Leeds United	42	1-3	3	5	37	19	8	6	7	28	27	51
6.	Ipswich Town	42	11	6	4	36	23	5	8	8	18	25	46
7.	Leicester City	42	9	9	3	29	24	4	10	7	19	27	45
8.	Manchester City	42	14	5	2	46	18	2	6	13	18	28	43
9.	Tottenham Hotspur	42	6	10	5	33	32	8	5	8	30	31	43
10.	Norwich City	42	10	5	6	33	26	6	5	10	25	32	42
11.	Everton	42	10	7	4	37	24	5	5	11	23	42	42
12.	Stoke City	42	8	5	8	25	24	7	6	8	23	26	41
13.	Middlesbrough	42	9	7	5	23	11	6	3	12	23	34	40
14.	Coventry City	42	6	9	6	22	22	7	5	9	25	35	40
15.	Newcastle United	42	11	4	6	51	26	4	5	12	20	36	39
16.	Aston Villa	42	11	8	2	32	17	0	9	12	19	42	39
17.	Arsenal	42	11	4	6	33	19	2	6	13	14	34	36
18.	West Ham United	42	10	5	6	26	23	3	5	13	22	48	36
19.	Birmingham City	42	11	5	5	36	26	2	2	17	21	49	33
20.	Wolverhampton W.	42	7	6	8	27	25	3	4	14	24	43	30
21.	Burnley	42	6	6	9	23	26	3	4	14	20	40	28
22.	Sheffield United	42	4	7	10	19	32	2	3	16	14	50	22

1976-77

Liverpool's tenth title was their first back-to-back success since 1922–23. Bob Paisley's men were almost irresistible, and only an FA Cup defeat against Manchester United denied them a treble of League, FA Cup and European Cup. Liverpool's main title adversaries in 1976–77 were from Manchester, but the blue half – City. A 0–0 draw with West Ham United clinched the Championship in the penultimate game.

DID YOU YOU KNOW THAT?
Liverpool have won four League and European cup doubles (UEFA Cup in 1972 and 1976, European Cup 1977 and 1984).

		P	W	D	L	F	A	W	D	L	F	A	Pts
1.	**Liverpool FC**	42	18	3	0	47	11	5	8	8	15	22	57
2.	Manchester City	42	15	5	1	38	13	6	9	6	22	21	56
3.	Ipswich Town	42	15	4	2	41	11	7	4	10	25	28	52
4.	Aston Villa	42	17	3	1	55	17	5	4	12	21	33	51
5.	Newcastle United	42	14	6	1	40	15	4	7	10	24	34	49
6.	Manchester United	42	12	6	3	41	22	6	5	10	30	40	47
7.	West Bromwich Albion	42	10	6	5	38	22	6	7	8	24	34	45
8.	Arsenal	42	11	6	4	37	20	5	5	11	27	39	43
9.	Everton	42	9	7	5	35	24	5	7	9	27	40	42
10.	Leeds United	42	8	8	5	28	26	7	4	10	20	25	42
11.	Leicester City	42	8	9	4	30	28	4	9	8	17	32	42
12.	Middlesbrough	42	11	6	4	25	14	3	7	11	15	31	41
13.	Birmingham City	42	10	6	5	38	25	3	6	12	25	36	38
14.	Queens Park Rangers	42	10	7	4	31	21	3	5	13	16	31	38
15.	Derby County	42	9	9	3	36	18	0	10	11	14	37	37
16.	Norwich City	42	12	4	5	30	23	2	5	14	17	41	37
17.	West Ham United	42	9	6	6	28	23	2	8	11	18	42	36
18.	Bristol City	42	8	7	6	25	19	3	6	12	13	29	35
19.	Coventry City	42	7	9	5	34	26	3	6	12	14	33	35
20.	Sunderland	42	9	5	7	29	16	2	7	12	17	38	34
21.	Stoke City	42	9	8	4	21	16	1	6	14	7	35	34
22.	Tottenham Hotspur	42	9	7	5	26	20	3	2	16	22	52	33

1978–79

Liverpool enjoyed two huge home victories in 1978–79, on the way to their fourth League title of the decade and 11th in all. It was 7–0 (Kenny Dalglish 2, Ray Kennedy, David Johnson 2, Phil Neal, Terry, McDermott) against Tottenham Hotspur and 6–0 (Dalglish 2, Johnson 2, Alan Kennedy, Ray Kennedy) over Norwich City. The Reds conceded just 16 goals, with only QPR, West Bromwich, Leeds and Everton scoring at Anfield, where they dropped only two points all season. Defending champions Nottingham Forest – who also took the Reds' European Cup that season, pushed Liverpool hard, but the Reds still finished eight points clear.

		P	W	D	L	F	A	W	D	L	F	A	Pts
1.	**Liverpool FC**	42	19	2	0	51	4	11	6	4	34	12	68
2.	Nottingham Forest	42	11	10	0	34	10	10	8	3	27	16	60
3.	West Bromwich Albion	42	13	5	3	38	15	11	6	4	34	20	59
4.	Everton	42	12	7	2	32	17	5	10	6	20	23	51
5.	Leeds United	42	11	4	6	41	25	7	10	4	29	27	50
6.	Ipswich Town	42	11	4	6	34	21	9	5	7	29	28	49
7.	Arsenal	42	11	8	2	37	18	6	6	9	24	30	48
8.	Aston Villa	42	8	9	4	37	26	7	7	7	22	23	46
9.	Manchester United	42	9	7	5	29	25	6	8	7	31	38	45
10.	Coventry City	42	11	7	3	41	29	3	9	9	17	39	44
11.	Tottenham Hotspur	42	7	8	6	19	25	6	7	8	29	36	41
12.	Middlesbrough	42	10	5	6	33	21	5	5	11	24	29	40
13.	Bristol City	42	11	6	4	34	19	4	4	13	13	32	40
14.	Southampton	42	9	10	2	35	20	3	6	12	12	33	40
15.	Manchester City	42	9	5	7	34	28	4	8	9	24	28	39
16.	Norwich City	42	7	10	4	29	19	0	13	8	22	38	37
17.	Bolton Wanderers	42	10	5	6	36	28	2	6	13	18	47	35
18.	Wolverhampton W.	42	10	4	7	26	26	3	4	14	18	42	34
19.	Derby County	42	8	5	8	25	25	2	6	13	19	46	31
20.	Queens Park Rangers	42	4	9	8	24	33	2	4	15	21	40	25
21.	Birmingham City	42	5	9	7	24	25	1	1	19	13	39	22
22.	Chelsea	42	3	5	13	23	42	2	5	14	21	50	20

1979-80

Liverpool won back-to-back Division One championships for the third time in 1979–80, using just 18 players in their 84 games over those two seasons. It was Liverpool's 12th League crown, four more than their nearest challengers, Arsenal. Manchester United who pushed Liverpool hardest all season, and defeated them 2–1 (Kenny Dalglish) at Old Trafford on 5 April. But the Reds held on to clinch the title by two points.

DID YOU KNOW THAT?
Liverpool didn't lose a League match at Anfield for a second consecutive season.

		P	W	D	L	F	A	W	D	L	F	A	Pts
1.	**Liverpool FC**	42	15	6	0	46	8	10	4	7	35	22	60
2.	Manchester United	42	17	3	1	43	8	7	7	7	22	27	58
3.	Ipswich Town	42	14	4	3	43	13	8	5	8	25	26	53
4.	Arsenal	42	8	10	3	24	12	10	6	5	28	24	52
5.	Nottingham Forest	42	16	4	1	44	11	4	4	13	19	32	48
6.	Wolverhampton W.	42	9	6	6	29	20	10	3	8	29	27	47
7.	Aston Villa	42	11	5	5	29	22	5	9	7	22	28	46
8.	Southampton	42	14	2	5	53	24	4	7	10	12	29	45
9.	Middlesbrough	42	11	7	3	31	14	5	5	11	19	30	44
10.	West Bromwich Albion	42	9	8	4	37	23	2	11	8	17	27	41
11.	Leeds United	42	10	7	4	30	17	3	7	11	16	33	40
12.	Norwich City	42	10	8	3	38	30	3	6	12	20	36	40
13.	Crystal Palace	42	9	9	3	26	13	3	7	11	15	37	40
14.	Tottenham Hotspur	42	11	5	5	30	22	4	5	12	22	40	40
15.	Coventry City	42	12	2	7	34	24	4	5	12	22	42	39
16.	Brighton & Hove A	42	8	8	5	25	20	3	7	11	22	37	37
17.	Manchester City	42	8	8	5	28	25	4	5	12	15	41	37
18.	Stoke City	42	9	4	8	27	26	4	6	11	17	32	36
19.	Everton	42	7	7	7	28	25	2	10	9	15	26	35
20.	Bristol City	42	6	6	9	22	30	3	7	11	15	36	31
21.	Derby County	42	9	4	8	36	29	2	4	15	11	38	30
22.	Bolton Wanderers	42	5	11	5	19	21	0	4	17	19	52	25

1981–82

Ipswich Town ran Liverpool a close second in the race for the 1981–82 Division One Championship. The Reds made a dire start to the season, winning just three of their first 11 League games and when Manchester City left Anfield with a 3–1 (Ronnie Whelan) on Boxing Day win, the Reds lay in 12th position. But the Kenny Dalglish–Ian Rush partnership ignited and the defence became secure. The Reds dropped just 12 points out of 75 on the way to their 13th League title

DID YOU KNOW THAT?

This was the first season with three points for a win.

		P	W	D	L	F	A	W	D	L	F	A	Pts
1.	**Liverpool FC**	42	14	3	4	39	14	12	6	3	41	18	87
2.	Ipswich Town	42	17	1	3	47	25	9	4	8	28	28	83
3.	Manchester United	42	12	6	3	27	9	10	6	5	32	20	78
4.	Tottenham Hotspur	42	12	4	5	41	26	8	7	6	26	22	71
5.	Arsenal	42	13	5	3	27	15	7	6	8	21	22	71
6.	Swansea City	42	13	3	5	34	16	8	3	10	24	35	69
7.	Southampton	42	15	2	4	49	30	4	7	10	23	37	66
8.	Everton	42	11	7	3	33	21	6	6	9	23	29	64
9.	West Ham United	42	9	10	2	42	29	5	6	10	24	28	58
10.	Manchester City	42	9	7	5	32	23	6	6	9	17	27	58
11.	Aston Villa	42	9	6	6	28	24	6	6	9	27	29	57
12.	Nottingham Forest	42	7	7	7	19	20	8	5	8	23	28	57
13.	Brighton & Hove A.	42	8	7	6	30	24	5	6	10	13	28	52
14.	Coventry City	42	9	4	8	31	24	4	7	10	25	38	50
15.	Notts County	42	8	5	8	32	33	5	3	13	29	36	47
16.	Birmingham City	42	8	6	7	29	25	2	8	11	24	36	44
17.	West Bromwich Albion	42	6	6	9	24	25	5	5	11	22	32	44
18.	Stoke City	42	9	2	10	27	28	3	6	12	17	35	44
19.	Sunderland	42	6	5	10	19	26	5	6	10	19	32	44
20.	Leeds United	42	6	11	4	23	20	4	1	16	16	41	42
21.	Wolverhampton W.	42	8	5	8	19	20	2	5	14	13	43	40
22.	Middlesbrough	42	5	9	7	20	24	3	6	12	14	28	39

1982–83

The strongest challenge to Liverpool in the 1982–83 League title race came from an unlikely source: Watford – owned by Elton John and managed by Graham Taylor – who were in their first season in Division One. Liverpool wanted to end the campaign in style for Bob Paisley, who had announced that he was retiring at the end of the season after ten years in charge. Liverpool won their 14th Championship by 11 points from Watford. In a season when no team lost more at home than they won, Liverpool was the only club to actually win more on the road than they lost. Paisley also lifted the League Cup to bring a fitting end to his Anfield career.

		P	W	D	L	F	A	W	D	L	F	A	Pts
1.	**Liverpool FC**	42	16	4	1	55	16	8	6	7	32	21	82
2.	Watford	42	16	2	3	49	20	6	3	12	25	37	71
3.	Manchester United	42	14	7	0	39	10	5	6	10	17	28	70
4.	Tottenham Hotspur	42	15	4	2	50	15	5	5	11	15	35	69
5.	Nottingham Forest	42	12	5	4	34	18	8	4	9	28	32	69
6.	Aston Villa	42	17	2	2	47	15	4	3	14	15	35	68
7.	Everton	42	13	6	2	43	19	5	4	12	23	29	64
8.	West Ham United	42	13	3	5	41	23	7	1	13	27	39	64
9.	Ipswich Town	42	11	3	7	39	23	4	10	7	25	27	58
10.	Arsenal	42	11	6	4	36	19	5	4	12	22	37	58
11.	West Bromwich Albion	42	11	5	5	35	20	4	7	10	16	29	57
12.	Southampton	42	11	5	5	36	22	4	7	10	18	36	57
13.	Stoke City	42	13	4	4	34	21	3	5	13	19	43	57
14.	Norwich City	42	10	6	5	30	18	4	6	11	22	40	54
15.	Notts County	42	12	4	5	37	25	3	3	15	18	46	52
16.	Sunderland	42	7	10	4	30	22	5	4	12	18	39	50
17.	Birmingham City	42	9	7	5	29	24	3	7	11	11	31	50
18.	Luton Town	42	7	7	7	34	33	5	6	10	31	51	49
19.	Coventry City	42	10	5	6	29	17	3	4	14	19	42	48
20.	Manchester City	42	9	5	7	26	23	4	3	14	21	47	47
21.	Swansea City	42	10	4	7	32	29	0	7	14	19	40	41
22.	Brighton & Hove A.	42	8	7	6	25	22	1	6	14	13	46	40

1983–84

Joe Fagan succeeded the retired Bob Paisley as manager and what a season it was for him as he guided Liverpool to a 15th League Championship title (their third in a row), a fourth European Cup and a second Football League Cup. Southampton pressed the Reds hard all season. However, whereas Liverpool lost six League games, the Saints lost nine. In the end Liverpool won the title by three points.

DID YOU KNOW THAT?
Manager Joe Fagan had to be persuaded to take a Jaguar as a club car in favour of his modest Ford.

		P	W	D	L	F	A	W	D	L	F	A	Pts
1.	**Liverpool FC**	42	14	5	2	50	12	8	9	4	23	20	80
2.	Southampton	42	15	4	2	44	17	7	7	7	22	21	77
3.	Nottingham Forest	42	14	4	3	47	17	8	4	9	29	28	74
4.	Manchester United	42	14	3	4	43	18	6	11	4	28	23	74
5.	Queens Park Rangers	42	14	4	3	37	12	8	3	10	30	25	73
6.	Arsenal	42	10	5	6	41	29	8	4	9	33	31	63
7.	Everton	42	9	9	3	21	12	7	5	9	23	30	62
8.	Tottenham Hotspur	42	11	4	6	31	24	6	6	9	33	41	61
9.	West Ham United	42	10	4	7	39	24	7	5	9	21	31	60
10.	Aston Villa	42	14	3	4	34	22	3	6	12	25	39	60
11.	Watford	42	9	7	5	36	31	7	2	12	32	46	57
12.	Ipswich Town	42	11	4	6	34	23	4	4	13	21	34	53
13.	Sunderland	42	8	9	4	26	18	5	4	12	16	35	52
14.	Norwich City	42	9	8	4	34	20	3	7	11	14	29	51
15.	Leicester City	42	11	5	5	40	30	2	7	12	25	38	51
16.	Luton Town	42	7	5	9	30	33	7	4	10	23	33	51
17.	West Bromwich Albion	42	10	4	7	30	25	4	5	12	18	37	51
18.	Stoke City	42	11	4	6	30	23	2	7	12	14	40	50
19.	Coventry City	42	8	5	8	33	33	5	6	10	24	44	50
20.	Birmingham City	42	7	7	7	19	18	5	5	11	20	32	48
21.	Notts County	42	6	7	8	31	36	4	4	13	19	36	41
22.	Wolverhampton W.	42	4	8	9	15	28	2	3	16	12	52	29

1985–86

The 1985–86 season saw a close battle for the title between Liverpool, under new player-manager Kenny Dalglish, and 1985 winners Everton. Liverpool won 3–2 (Dalglish, Ian Rush, Steve McMahon) at Goodison Park in September, but lost 2–0 at Anfield in February. The Reds then won 11 and drew one of their remaining 12 League games, taking 34 out of 36 points, to claim their 16th Championship, and clinched it with a 1–0 (Dalglish) victory at Chelsea. Liverpool also became the third club in the 20th century to do the League Championship and FA Cup double, beating Everton 3–1 (Rush 2, Craig Johnston) in the FA Cup final at Wembley.

		P	W	D	L	F	A	W	D	L	F	A	Pts
1.	**Liverpool FC**	42	16	4	1	58	14	10	6	5	31	23	88
2.	Everton	42	16	3	2	54	18	10	5	6	33	23	86
3.	West Ham United	42	17	2	2	48	16	9	4	8	26	24	84
4.	Manchester United	42	12	5	4	35	12	10	5	6	35	24	76
5.	Sheffield Wednesday	42	13	6	2	36	23	8	4	9	27	31	73
6.	Chelsea	42	12	4	5	32	27	8	7	6	25	29	71
7.	Arsenal	42	13	5	3	29	15	7	4	10	20	32	69
8.	Nottingham Forest	42	11	5	5	38	25	8	6	7	31	28	68
9.	Luton Town	42	12	6	3	37	15	6	6	9	24	29	66
10.	Tottenham Hotspur	42	12	2	7	47	25	7	6	8	27	27	65
11.	Newcastle United	42	12	5	4	46	31	5	7	9	21	41	63
12.	Watford	42	11	6	4	40	22	5	5	11	29	40	59
13.	Queens Park Rangers	42	12	3	6	33	20	3	4	14	20	44	52
14.	Southampton	42	10	6	5	32	18	2	4	15	19	44	46
15.	Manchester City	42	7	7	7	25	26	4	5	12	18	31	45
16.	Aston Villa	42	7	6	8	27	28	3	8	10	24	39	44
17.	Coventry City	42	6	5	10	31	35	5	5	11	17	36	43
18.	Oxford United	42	7	7	7	34	27	3	5	13	28	53	42
19.	Leicester City	42	7	8	6	35	35	3	4	14	19	41	42
20.	Ipswich Town	42	8	5	8	20	24	3	3	15	12	31	41
21.	Birmingham City	42	5	2	14	13	25	3	3	15	17	48	29
22.	West Bromwich Albion	42	3	8	10	21	36	1	4	16	14	53	24

1987–88

The 1987–88 season brought Liverpool their 17th Football League Championship. Throughout the campaign the Reds were awesome winning 26 and losing just twice, to Everton and Nottingham Forest, in 40 League games. The defence was Scrooge-like, conceding only 24 goals, nine at home – where they went undefeated. Liverpool strolled to the title by a massive nine points from Manchester United, with Forest a further eight behind in third place

DID YOU KNOW THAT?
Liverpool's dreams of another domestic Double were dashed by underdogs Wimbledon, 1–0, in the FA Cup final.

		P	W	D	L	F	A	W	D	L	F	A	Pts
1.	**Liverpool FC**	40	15	5	0	49	9	11	7	2	38	15	90
2.	Manchester United	40	14	5	1	41	17	9	7	4	30	21	81
3.	Nottingham Forest	40	11	7	2	40	17	9	6	5	27	22	73
4.	Everton	40	14	4	2	34	11	5	9	6	19	16	70
5.	Queens Park Rangers	40	12	4	4	30	14	7	6	7	18	24	67
6.	Arsenal	40	11	4	5	35	16	7	8	5	23	23	66
7.	Wimbledon	40	8	9	3	32	20	6	6	8	26	27	57
8.	Newcastle United	40	9	6	5	32	23	5	8	7	23	30	56
9.	Luton Town	40	11	6	3	40	21	3	5	12	17	37	53
10.	Coventry City	40	6	8	6	23	25	7	6	7	23	28	53
11.	Sheffield Wednesday	40	10	2	8	27	30	5	6	9	25	36	53
12.	Southampton	40	6	8	6	27	26	6	6	8	22	27	50
13.	Tottenham Hotspur	40	9	5	6	26	23	3	6	11	12	25	47
14.	Norwich City	40	7	5	8	26	26	5	4	11	14	26	45
15.	Derby County	40	6	7	7	18	17	4	6	10	17	28	43
16.	West Ham United	40	6	9	5	23	21	3	6	11	17	31	42
17.	Charlton Athletic	40	7	7	6	23	21	2	8	10	15	31	42
18.	Chelsea	40	7	11	2	24	17	2	4	14	26	51	42
19.	Portsmouth	40	4	8	8	21	27	3	6	11	15	39	35
20.	Watford	40	4	5	11	15	24	3	6	11	12	27	32
21.	Oxford United	40	5	7	8	24	34	1	6	13	20	46	31

1989-90

In 1989–90 Liverpool won their 18th Football League Championship title. Division One had been reduced to 20 clubs, so the campaign consisted of just 38 games. The Reds were, again dominant, especially at Anfield, where they won 13 and drew five of 19 matches. Aston Villa were the runners-up, finishing nine points behind Liverpool, and they played out a pair of 1–1 draw with Reds, John Barnes scoring at Villa Park, Peter Beardsley at Anfield.

DID YOU KNOW THAT?
Eight London clubs were in Division One, while Lancashire had only four, Yorkshire one and the North-east none.

		P	W	D	L	F	A	W	D	L	F	A	Pts
1.	**Liverpool FC**	38	13	5	1	38	15	10	5	4	40	22	79
2.	Aston Villa	38	13	3	3	36	20	8	4	7	21	18	70
3.	Tottenham Hotspur	38	12	1	6	35	24	7	5	7	24	23	63
4.	Arsenal	38	14	3	2	38	11	4	5	10	16	27	62
5.	Chelsea	38	8	7	4	31	24	8	5	6	27	26	60
6.	Everton	38	14	3	2	40	16	3	5	11	17	30	59
7.	Southampton	38	10	5	4	40	27	5	5	9	31	36	55
8.	Wimbledon	38	5	8	6	22	23	8	8	3	25	17	55
9.	Nottingham Forest	38	9	4	6	31	21	6	5	8	24	26	54
10.	Norwich City	38	7	10	2	24	14	6	4	9	20	28	53
11.	Queens Park Rangers	38	9	4	6	27	22	4	7	8	18	22	50
12.	Coventry City	38	11	2	6	24	25	3	5	11	15	34	49
13.	Manchester United	38	8	6	5	26	14	5	3	11	20	33	48
14.	Manchester City	38	9	4	6	26	21	3	8	8	17	31	48
15.	Crystal Palace	38	8	7	4	27	23	5	2	12	15	43	48
16.	Derby County	38	9	1	9	29	21	4	6	9	14	19	46
17.	Luton Town	38	8	8	3	24	18	2	5	12	19	39	43
18.	Sheffield Wednesday	38	8	6	5	21	17	3	4	12	14	34	43
19.	Charlton Athletic	38	4	6	9	18	25	3	3	13	13	32	30
20.	Millwall	38	4	6	9	23	25	1	5	13	16	40	26

CHAPTER

3

LIVERPOOL LEGENDS

There are very few clubs in the world where if you have starred in a World Cup final, or are regularly considered amongst the best players or managers anywhere in the world, but you still can't find find a place in the top 16 legends. That is the case here if you looking to read about football greats such as Xabi Alonso, Javier Mascherano, Ray Clemence, Peter Beardsley or Mark Lawrenson, Gerard Houllier and Rafael Benitez.

To crack the Liverpool list of legends, you have to be more than a bit special and the 16 players and managers who appear in this section fit that criterion. All have given Liverpool FC fantastic service and every one of these legends has made at least 300 appearances for the club.

To reach the final 16, it was decided that only the last 60-odd years should be considered and players who earned legendary status at Anfield were chosen ahead of some whose careers in total may have been more storied. These potted biographies cover mainly the legends' career at Liverpool, their finest hours at Anfield and all are complemented by a statistics box on their time at Anfield. And, just in case you were wondering, these Liverpool Legends appear in alphabetical order.

John Barnes

While the number 7 shirt is synonymous with Kenny Dalglish, Liverpool's number 10 will always belong to John Barnes. His talent enthralled those who flocked to see him in full flight, breaking down racial barriers as the first high profile black player to grace Anfield in the 1980s.

Along with the likes of Lawrie Cunningham, Cyrille Regis and Viv Anderson, Barnes was part of an exciting group of players that were a catalyst for change at a time when racial abuse was prevalent from the stands.

Barnes arrived for £900,000 from Watford in 1987 to feature alongside fellow attackers John Aldridge and Peter Beardsley helping Liverpool play the sort of football that ensured a packed house every week.

A front row seat in the Kemlyn Road or Paddock was the hottest ticket in town and Barnes wasted no time in making his mark on his new side. A sublime free-kick against Oxford on his home debut announced himself to the Kop and

that was followed by a stunning solo goal against QPR.

The infamous banana-throwing incident in the Merseyside derby at Goodison Park would have perhaps knocked lesser players off their stride yet Barnes dealt with it the only way he knew how – with a back-heel to remove it from the pitch.

Barnes' fleet of foot propelled Liverpool to their 17th league title – which included a 29-match unbeaten run and it was no surprise he walked away with both the 1987 and 1998 player of the year awards.

His first season was explosive but 'Digger' continued to entertain at a high level over the next nine years and success in the 1989 FA Cup final against Everton made up for the heartbreak against Wimbledon a year previously.

Barnes helped secure another league title in 1990 and scored 22 league goals in a campaign where he landed the Football Writers' Association Footballer of the Year award.

His influence on and off the field was crucial as well, with youngsters Robbie Fowler, Jamie Redknapp and Steve McManaman all learning from him as they made their first steps in professional football.

He dazzled on the mic as well, with his raps on New Order's World in Motion and the Anfield Rap as entertaining as his dribbles down the wing for the Reds.

While a serious injury hampered him in his final days as a Liverpool player, he reinvented himself as an accustomed centre midfielder and he led out the side for the 1996 FA Cup final.

Anyone with any doubt as to Barnes' qualities would do well to listen to the words of Bob Paisley, who once claimed Digger would walk into any of the great Liverpool sides. Praise indeed.

DID YOU KNOW THAT?

Barnes competed in Strictly Come Dancing in October 2007 and was also the first male celebrity to receive a 10 from the judges.

For the Record

Born: 07 November 1963, Kingston, Jamaica.
Country: England, 79 caps, 11 goals
Liverpool appearances: 407
Liverpool goals: 108
Liverpool debut: A v Arsenal, 15 August 1987

Ian Callaghan

Ian Callaghan wore the Liver bird on his chest 857 times during a trophy-laden 18 years at the club. His trophy haul is majestic – six league titles, two European Cups, two UEFA Cups, one UEFA Super Cup and two FA Cups. Quite simply, Liverpool's leading appearance maker needs no introduction.

The Toxteth boy was the only survivor as the club was transformed from the sleeping giant of Second Division outfit to European heavyweights. He was there every step on that fairytale journey, winning almost every honour imaginable. A true gentlemen, he was booked just once during his Anfield career, commanding the respect of fellow professionals, team-mates and fans alike.

He initially joined as an apprentice but it was not long until his obvious talent and dedication shone through enough to put him on a path to greatness with the senior side. After just four outings for the reserves, he was thrust into first team action in April 1960 at home to Bristol Rovers.

It was quite an ask – not to mention the fact he had the added burden of replacing Liverpool idol Billy Liddell. Such a task would have consumed others but Cally rose to the challenge and at 17, turned in a performance that went down in folklore – he was applauded off the pitch by both teams, the crowd and the referee.

That was just the start of a meteoric rise that would result in him going down as one of the club's greatest ever players. Initially a winger, he reinvented himself in later years as a commanding presence in the middle of the park, marrying searing pace with incredible stamina.

His breakthrough campaign came in 1961-62, as he became a first team regular, supplying the ammunition for the prolific Hunt and St John in Liverpool's promotion season.

The fact he was one of the first names on Bill Shankly's team-sheets during the glory years in the 60s is testament to his standing among the club's legends, displaying the unwavering fighting qualities he would need in the early 70s.

A cartilage operation rendered the 70-71 season largely a write off and question marks gathered over his long term future in the game. But Callaghan came back fighting fit and emerged as a central midfield battler.

In 73-74, a world away from his teen years and his first steps on the big stage, Callaghan overtook Liddell's record of 492 appearances, scored his one and only senior hat-trick, helped with the FA Cup and also became the first Liverpool player to scoop the Football Writers' Footballer of the Year award.

Cally's longevity meant he was still part of the team that conquered Europe for the first time in 1977 – quite a feat for a man who had featured in Liverpool's first match in the competition 13 years previously. A true legend of the club, Callaghan joined for a £10 signing-on fee in 1960. Talk about money well spent.

DID YOU KNOW THAT?
Callaghan is one of only three English footballers to have a World Cup and a European Cup winner's medal.

For the Record
Born: 10 April 1942, Toxteth, Liverpool.
Country: England, 4 caps.
Liverpool appearances: 857
Liverpool goals: 68
Liverpool debut: H v Bristol Rovers, 16 April 1960

Jamie Carragher

Jamie Carragher was born on 28 January 1978 in Bootle, Merseyside. Already on Liverpool's books, Carragher attended the FA School of Excellence at Lilleshall. In 1996 he was a member of Liverpool's FA Youth Cup winning team and in October of that year, he signed professional terms with the Reds. He made his Liverpool first-team debut on 8 January 1997 as a substitute in the Reds' 2–1 defeat at Middlesbrough in the League Cup. Three days later he made his Premier League debut at Anfield, a 0–0 draw with West Ham United. A week later Carragher scored in front of the Kop in Liverpool's 3–0 win over Aston Villa.

Carragher began to command a regular starting position in 1997–98, but, unfortunately for him, manager Roy Evans could not decide what his best position was, so he was played at left-back, right-back, centre-half and defensive midfielder. But Carrragher's no-nonsense style soon made him a fans' favourite. Under new boss Gerard Houllier in 2000–01, he collected his first senior medals, and did so in some style as Liverpool won five trophies: the League Cup, FA Cup, UEFA Cup, Charity Shield and European Super Cup.

Unfortunately, two serious injuries put his career on hold. Carragher missed out on a place in the England squad for the 2002 FIFA World Cup finals in Japan and South Korea because of a knee injury. In 2003 he broke his leg in a match against Blackburn Rovers. But Carragher recovered from his injuries and reclaimed his place in the team.

When Rafael Benitez replaced Houllier in the summer of 2004 it marked a turning point in Carragher's career. Benitez moved him to centre-half, where he flourished alongside Sami Hyypia in a dominating partnership. Indeed, their performances at the heart of the Liverpool defence was the foundation upon which the Reds built their fifth UEFA Champions League winning squad in 2005. Carragher went on to captain Liverpool in their 2005 UEFA Super Cup win over CSKA Moscow and, in 2006, he collected another FA Cup winners' medal. He enjoyed a run in the England team and went to the World Cup finals in Germany and he appeared in four matches, including the quarter-final against Portugal, when he had the misfortune of having a penalty shoot-out effort saved.

He retired from international football in 2006–07, but his club career continued to thrive. Carragher passed Ian Callaghan's Liverpool record of 89 European appearances in May 2007 and soon became the first Red to reach a century in European competition. He made his 700th first-team appearance for the club during the 2012–13 Premier League campaign and retired at the end of the season.

DID YOU KNOW THAT?

Carragher came out of international retirement in 2010 and played in two matches at the World Cup in South Africa. He retired again after the tournament with 38 caps to his name.

For the Record

Born: 28 January 1978, Bootle, Merseyside
Country: England, 38 apps, 0 goals
Liverpool appearances: 737
Liverpool goals: 5
Liverpool debut: A v Middlesbrough, 8 January 1997,
   League Cup

Kenny Dalglish, MBE

Kenny Dalglish was born on 4 March 1951 in Dalmarnock, Glasgow. He arrived at Anfield from Celtic on 10 August 1977 as a replacement for Kevin Keegan. "King Kenny" cost Liverpool a then British record £440,000, and although many players fail to live up to the "most expensive player" tag, there is no doubt he did.

In Kenny's first season at Anfield, the Reds won the European Cup for the second consecutive year, thanks to his superb chip over the FC Bruges goalkeeper in the final. In 1980 Ian Rush signed for Liverpool, and the Dalglish-Rush partnership was unstoppable. Dalglish was the creative genius; Rush the lethal marksman. Liverpool dominated the 1980s, winning more trophies in one decade than any club had previously managed. But Dalglish was much more than a creator, as 172 goals in 515 games proves.

In 1985 Kenny, who had been awarded the MBE a year earlier, was appointed Liverpool's first ever player-manager and many people in the game considered it to be a huge gamble. However, this notion was completely dismissed when Liverpool won the League and FA Cup Double (only the fifth club ever to do so) in Dalglish's first season in charge. An astute man, Kenny also had an eye for a player, and when Ian Rush left the club for Juventus in 1987, Dalglish bought John Aldridge, John Barnes and Peter Beardsley. The Liverpool team that captured the League Championship in the 1987–88 season is regarded by many as being among the best that Liverpool have ever produced. Aldridge (29), Barnes (18) and Beardsley (17) scored 64 goals between them, while the Reds lost only two League games.

Following the Hillsborough Disaster on 15 April 1989,

in which 96 Liverpool fans died, Dalglish spent much time attending funerals and trying to comfort the bereaved. In 1990 Liverpool again won the title, but the stress brought on by the disaster was clearly taking its toll. On 22 February 1991, just a few days after a famous 4–4 FA Cup draw with Everton, Dalglish shocked the football world by resigning. During his times as a player and manager Liverpool won eight League Championships, three European Cups, two FA Cups, five League Cups (including 2012) and four Charity Shields.

Kenny replaced Roy Hodgson in January 2011, but made way again after leading the club to League Cup glory in 2012.

DID YOU KNOW THAT?
Kenny Dalglish is one of only two men to manage two League Championship winning clubs since World War 2. He won three Division One titles at Liverpool and the Premier League with Blackburn Rovers (Brian Clough is the other).

For the Record

Born: 4 March 1951, Dalmarnock, Glasgow, Scotland
Player (Liverpool 1977–88)
Country: Scotland, 102 apps, 30 goals
Liverpool appearances: 515
Liverpool goals: 172
Liverpool debut: N (Wembley) v Manchester United, 13 August 1977, FA Charity Shield
Manager (1985–1991, 2011–12)
Liverpool record: P371, W215, D93, L63
Liverpool major honours: League (3): 1986, 1988, 1990; FA Cup (2): 1986, 1989; League Cup (1): 2012

Robbie Fowler

Robbie Fowler was born on 9 April 1975 in Toxteth, Liverpool. He signed schoolboy forms with Liverpool, then became a YTS trainee with the club, before turning professional on his 17th birthday. On 22 September 1993 he made his debut for the Reds, scoring in a 3–1 away win over Fulham in the first leg of the first round of the Coca-Cola Cup. Two weeks later, Liverpool beat Fulham 5–0 at Anfield in the second leg with Fowler netting all five. He scored his first League hat-trick, against Southampton at Anfield on 30 October 1993.

In November 1993 Fowler made his England Under-21 debut against San Marino and celebrated by scoring England's opener after only three minutes. At the end of that 1993–94 season, he was Liverpool's leading scorer with 18 goals and in each of the following two seasons he broke the 30-goal barrier. In 1995 Robbie won his first trophy with Liverpool, the League Cup, and that year, and again in 1996, he was voted PFA Young Player of the Year. Fowler's goalscoring exploits for the Reds during the 1990s earned him iconic status among Anfield fans, who nicknamed him "God". In 1994–95 Fowler scored a hat-trick against Arsenal in only 4 minutes and 33 seconds – easily the fastest in Premier League history – and, on 14 December 1996, he found the net four times against Middlesbrough at Anfield to record his 100th goal for the Reds, achieving the milestone in one game fewer than his hero Ian Rush.

In 1998 he suffered two serious injuries, which restricted him to a handful of games, and missed the 1998 World Cup Finals in France.

Fowler left Liverpool on 30 November 2001 after 330 games and 171 goals. His devotion to the Reds can be seen from the fact that he went to the 2005 Champions League final in Istanbul as a fan. Further proof came on 27 January 2006, when after spells at Leeds United and Manchester City, Fowler returned to Anfield, where he stayed until the end of the 2006–07 season.

Fowler enjoyed one of his finest moments in a red shirt during this return to the club when he overtook Kenny Dalglish to become Liverpool's fifth-highest goalscorer in their history. The Scot had persuaded a young Fowler to sign for the club by giving the teenage Everton fan lifts home – and it had already become patently clear what the Scot had seen in Fowler.

And when "God", as he would become known by Liverpool fans, opened the scoring in a 2-0 win at West Brom in Aprill 2006, it meant he had overtaken Dalglish's record of 172 goals for the club. "To get anywhere near Kenny is an achievement which I am greatly proud of," beamed Fowler. Although he wasn't in the 16 for the 2007 Champions League final that year, he received a runners-up medal having played earlier in the competition.

DID YOU KNOW THAT?

Fowler went on to play for Cardiff City and Blackburn Rovers, then North Queensland Fury and Perth Glory in Australia.

For the Record

Born: 9 April 1975, Toxteth, Liverpool

Country: England, 26 apps, 7 goals

Liverpool appearances: 369

Liverpool goals: 183

Liverpool debut: A v Fulham, 22 September 1993,
League Cup

Steven Gerrard, MBE

Steven Gerrard was born in Whiston, on the outskirts of Liverpool, on 30 May 1980. After playing for Whiston Juniors, he joined the Liverpool Academy at the age of nine, though was not an immediate success, and was overlooked by England schoolboys. He signed his first professional contract in October 1997.

A little more than a year later, the 18-year-old Gerrard made his Liverpool debut in a 2–0 defeat of Blackburn Rovers at Anfield. Injury problems hampered his advancement, but he still scored his first goal in the Premiership in December 1999, in a 4–1 (Sami Hyppia, Danny Murphy and David Thompson also scoring) defeat of Sheffield Wednesday at Anfield. Having already played for England at Under-18 and Under-21 levels, at the end of the 1999–2000 season, England manager Kevin Keegan called him into the full squad and in May he made his debut against Ukraine. Gerrard made the England squad for Euro 2000, and had one substitute appearance in the finals.

Gerrard's star was on the rise and, in 2001, he collected his first club medals, as Liverpool swept the FA Cup, League Cup, UEFA Cup (he scored in the 5–4 extra time defeat of Alaves in the final in Rotterdam), Charity Shield and UEFA Super Cup. He also received his first honour, the PFA Young Player of the Year. Gerrard was one of three Liverpool players (Michael Owen, 3, and Emile Heskey being the others) who scored against Germany in Munich in England's 5–1 win in September 2001, his first goal for his country. Sadly an injury denied him a place in the 2002 World Cup finals.

In 2003, Gerrard was appointed Liverpool captain, and he proved to be an inspirational leader. In the Reds' 2005

UEFA Champions League-winning campaign, he was outstanding, and scored vital goals at every stage, including the first in the amazing fightback against AC Milan in the final at Istanbul's Attaturk Stadium. When Liverpool won the match after a penalty shoot-out, Gerrard became the second-youngest skipper – after Marseille's Didier Deschamps in 1993 – to be presented with the Champions League trophy. In 2005–06, he helped Liverpool win the FA Cup, scoring twice in the final against West Ham United. And, to cap another outstanding season, he was named PFA Player of the Year.

Liverpool's most capped international with 102, Gerrard captained England at both the 2010 FIFA World Cup and the 2012 UEFA European Championships. His performances for Roy Hodgson's team were so good he was the only England player named to the UEFA 2012 Team of the Tournament.

DID YOU KNOW THAT?

Gerrard has been on Liverpool's books since the age of eight, and was the same height as Michael Owen until he was 15, at which point he went through a growth spurt.

For the Record

Born: 30 May 1980, Whiston, Merseyside
Country: England, 102 apps, 19 goals
Liverpool appearances: 629
Liverpool goals: 159
Liverpool debut: H v Blackburn Rovers,
   29 September 1998, League

Alan Hansen

Alan Hansen was born on 13 June 1955 in Sauchie, Scotland. In 1973 he joined his brother John at Partick Thistle and played more than 100 games for "The Jags", impressing many teams north and south of the border with his calm, cool, assured displays in defence. Leading the suitors were Liverpool and, in May 1977, they paid £100,000 to sign him.

His first-team debut came on 24 September 1977, in a 1–0 (Terry McDermott) Division One win over Derby County at Anfield. Although Hansen appeared only 18 times in the League in season 1977–78 – a campaign in which Liverpool finished runners-up in both Division One and the League Cup to Nottingham Forest – he did end up with a European Cup winners medal following the 1–0 defeat of Club Brugge at Wembley (Kenny Dalglish). In 1978–79, Hansen established himself as a regular in the heart of the Liverpool defence and helped the Reds regain the First Division Championship. He also made his full international debut for Scotland.

In 1979–80 Hansen won his third League Championship winners' medal as the Reds retained their title. There was no League glory for Liverpool in 1980–81, but Hansen did end the season with his second European Cup winners' medal, following the 1–0 (Alan Kennedy) defeat of Real Madrid in Paris, and with a League Cup winners' medal when he scored the match-winner against West Ham United at Villa Park in the replayed final.

Hansen's defensive partnership with Mark Lawrenson blossomed as Liverpool continued to dominated at home and abroad. He won his fourth League crown in 1982 and following the season, travelled to Spain with Scotland for the World Cup finals, where he played in all three of his country's matches. He won League Cup winners medals in both 1983 and 1984, as Liverpool beat Manchester United 2–1 (Alan Kennedy, Ronnie Whelan) in 1983 and Everton in a replay at Maine Road, Manchester (1–0 – Graeme Souness), a year later. Hansen also won a third European Cup medal in 1984 after AS Roma were beaten on penalties in Rome.

Another proud moment for Hansen came in 1986, when, as captain, he lifted the FA Cup at Wembley to add to the 1985–86 League Championship, making Liverpool only the third team to win the Double in the twentieth century. Alan retired in 1990 after 616 appearances and 14 goals for the Reds. He won eight League Championships, two FA Cups, three League Cups, five FA Charity Shields and three European Cups with Liverpool.

Since retiring Alan has been a regular on the BBC's *Match of the Day* programme, a role, he noted, which has seen him stopped more in the street than he ever was as a player.

DID YOU KNOW THAT?

Despite being recognised as one of the best defenders in the world in 1986, Hansen was omitted from the 1986 Scotland World Cup squad by manager Alex Ferguson.

For the Record

Born: 13 June 1955, Sauchie, Scotland
Country: Scotland, 26 apps, 0 goals
Liverpool appearances: 620
Liverpool goals: 14
Liverpool debut: H v Derby County,
    24 September 1997, League

Steve Heighway

Steve Heighway was born in Dublin on 25 November 1947. His path to greatness was somewhat unorthodox because he did not attract any real interest until he was in his 20s. In 1970, when already 22 years old, Steve was studying at the University of Warwick, doing his finals for a degree in ecomomics, whilst also playing for champions-elect Skelmersdale United in the Cheshire County League, where he was spotted by a Liverpool scout and quickly signed. On 22 September 1970 Heighway made his Reds debut against Mansfield Town in a League Cup tie at Anfield.

Heighway was a strong, athletic and quick winger who provided many pinpoint crosses into the box for Kevin Keegan and John Toshack to put away. He helped Liverpool to reach the 1971 FA Cup final, where League champions Arsenal were aiming to become only the second club to do the Double in the twentieth century. Heighway played well for the Reds on a humid afternoon and was as energetic as anyone the pitch. Early in extra time, he raced down the wing and cut inside Pat Rice before firing past Bob Wilson into the Arsenal net. However, Arsenal scored twice to deny Steve an FA Cup winners' medal in his first season as a professional footballer.

In 1972–73, Heighway won the first of four League Championship winners' medals with the Reds and the first two UEFA Cup winners' medal. He had an outstanding season in 1973–74 and his performances played a big part in Liverpool returning to Wembley for the FA Cup final for an encounter with Newcastle United. This time Liverpool lifted the Cup after a 3–0 victory, with Heighway and Keegan (2) the goalscorers. In 1975–76, he completed a second

League and UEFA Cup double, while the following season saw Liverpool conquer almost all before them to just miss out on the treble of of League, FA Cup and European Cup, going down 2–1 (Jimmy Case) to Manchester United in the FA Cup final. In the European Cup final, though, Heighway set up two of Liverpool's three goals in their 3–1 (Terry McDermott, Tommy Smith, Phil Neal) victory over Borussia Moenchengladbach in Rome.

He won two more European Cup winners' medals (1978 and 1981), another League Championship (1979), the European Super Cup (1978) and a League Cup winners' medal (1981). In 1981 Heighway left Anfield, having made 475 appearances for the club, scoring 76 goals, as well as winning 34 caps for the Republic of Ireland. Heighway returned to Anfield in 1989, where he took up coaching role at the Academy. He retired in 2007, after winning the FA Youth Cup for the third time in 11 years.

DID YOU KNOW THAT?

It was Bob Paisley's sons who first spotted Steve Heighway playing for Skelmersdale United against South Liverpool in 1970 and they recommended him to their father.

For the Record

Born: 25 November 1947, Dublin, Republic of Ireland
Country: Republic of Ireland, 34 apps, 14 goals
Liverpool appearances: 475
Liverpool goals: 76
Liverpool debut: H v Mansfield Town,
   22 September 1970, League Cup

Emlyn Hughes, OBE

Emlyn Hughes was born on 28 August 1947 in Barrow-in-Furness. Hughes came from a sporting family – his father was former Barrow and Great Britain rugby league star Fred Hughes, both his brother and uncle were rugby league professionals, while one of his aunts was an England hockey international. In February 1967 Bill Shankly signed the 19-year-old Hughes from Blackpool for £65,000. He had only played 31 League and Cup games for the Tangerines, but his strength, skill and bravery led Bill Shankly to boldly declare, "This boy is the future captain of England." How right Shankly was! Hughes went on to win 62 England caps, 59 of them while a Liverpool player, and he captained his country on 23 occasions.

Hughes made his debut for the Reds on 4 March 1967 in a 2–1 (Chris Lawler, Roger Hunt) First Division home win over Stoke City. He proved to be a major asset to the Liverpool side, adding a new dimension to their play. He could break up an opposition attack and then surge upfield, sometimes finishing a move off with a cannonball shot. His team-mates quickly named him "Crazy Horse", because his infectious enthusiasm for the game lit up the Liverpool dressing room, while out on the pitch he just never seemed to tire. He played for Liverpool at full-back, centre-half and in midfield and earned a place as one of the greatest of all Liverpool captains, the first to hold aloft the European Cup, after the 3–1 (Terry McDermott, Tommy Smith, Phil Neal) win over Borussia Moenchengladbach in Rome in 1977.

Hughes won his first England cap against Holland on 5 November 1969 in a 1–0 win in Amsterdam. In 1970 he was a non-playing member of the England squad that travelled to Mexico for the World Cup Finals. In 1974 he replaced Bobby Moore as England captain, but with England failing to qualify for three consecutive major tournaments, Emlyn never played for his country in a World Cup or European Championship finals.

Emlyn won his first medal with Liverpool in 1973 when the Reds lifted the First Division Championship, and that same season he added a UEFA Cup winners' medal. In all, he won four League Championships, two European Cups, two UEFA Cups and one FA Cup. His many personal accolades included the Football Writers' Association Footballer of the Year in 1977 and OBE for his services to football in 1983.

In August 1979, after 665 games and 49 goals for Liverpool, Hughes joined Wolverhampton Wanderers for £90,000, going on to success with Wolves, in 1980, in the one trophy he never won during his Anfield days, the League Cup. Sadly, Emlyn Hughes died of a brain tumour on 9 November 2004 at his home in Sheffield.

DID YOU KNOW THAT?
Emlyn Hughes was a captain on the BBC TV show *A Question of Sport* from 1979 to 1981 and again from 1984 to 1988.

For the Record

Born: 28 August 1947, Barrow-in-Furness, Cumbria
Died: 9 November 2004, Sheffield
Country: England, 62 apps, 4 goals
Liverpool appearances: 665
Liverpool goals: 49
Liverpool debut: H v Stoke City, 4 March 1967, League

Roger Hunt, MBE

Roger Hunt, nicknamed "Sir Roger" by the Kop, was born on 20 July 1938 in Golborne, England. He began his career at Stockton Heath, moved on to Bury, Stockton Heath for a second spell, Devizes Town and Stockton Heath once again before impressing Liverpool scout Bill Jones who had no hesitation in persuading Liverpool manager, Phil Taylor, to bring him to Anfield on a free transfer in July 1958. He made his debut for the Reds on 9 September 1959 in a 2–0 win over Scunthorpe United in Division Two, scoring in the 64th minute of the game (a thunderous strike from 20 yards). Hunt only got his chance in the starting line-up as a direct result of the absence of Liverpool legend Billy Liddell. In season 1961–62 he struck up a lethal partnership with new arrival Ian St John and the dynamic duo helped Liverpool to win promotion to Division One with Hunt scoring 41 League goals in 41 League games (he missed one League match), including five hat-tricks. His exploits brought him to the attention of England manager Walter Winterbottom who gave him his first cap on 4 April 1962, scoring in a 3-1 win over Austria at Wembley. He was in England's 1962 England World Cup finals squad in Chile, but did not play.

Hunt was Liverpool's leading scorer for eight straight seasons, 1961–62 to 1968–69, and in 1963–64, grabbed 31 goals as the Reds claimed their sixth Football League title He was instrumental again the championship season of 1965–66, when he scored 30 times. On 22 August 1964, Hunt scored the opening goal in the 11th minute of a Division One match against Arsenal at Anfield, a game the Reds would go on to win 3–2. This goal was notably, mainly because it was the first ever goal seen on the BBC

Television's new football highlights programme, *Match of the Day*. In 1964-65, he played a pivotal role in Liverpool's first FA Cup triumph. He scored four times en route to the Wembley showdown against Don Revie's Leeds United. After 90 minutes of stalemate, Hunt scored three minutes into extra time to give Liverpool the lead. Ian St John scored the winner, as the Reds triumphed 2–1.

Hunt played in all six of England's games in the 1966 World Cup finals, scoring three times in the first round group stage, and helping them to win the Jules Rimet trophy. In all, he made 34 appearances for his country and scored 18 times. Eleven months after breaking the club goalscoring record, Hunt said farewell to Anfield. He had amassed 492 appearances and 286 goals (including 254 in the League – still the record) in a Liverpool jersey. Hunt joined Bolton Wanderers and scored 24 goals in 76 games for them.

DID YOU KNOW THAT?

In Liverpool's 2–1 victory over Chelsea on 18 January 1969, when Roger Hunt broke Gordon Hodgson's club scoring record, the other Reds goal came from a future manager Roy Evans.

For the Record

Born: 20 July 1938, Golborne, Lancashire
Country: England, 34 apps, 18 goals
Liverpool appearances: 492
Liverpool goals: 286
Liverpool debut: H v Scunthorpe United,
  9 September 1959, League

Kevin Keegan, OBE

Kevin Keegan was born on 14 February 1951 in Armthorpe, Yorkshire. As a teenager, Keegan was rejected by his local team, Doncaster Rovers, but Scunthorpe United recognised he had talent and signed him. Keegan made 120 appearances for "The Iron" before moving to Liverpool in May 1971 for £33,000. On 14 August 1971 he made a spectacular debut for the Reds, scoring after just 12 minutes in a 3–1 home win over Nottingham Forest (Tommy Smith and Emlyn Hughes also netted). Speaking of his new recruit, Bill Shankly described the £33,000 fee as "robbery with violence", and could not believe his luck at having acquired such a bargain.

For the next six seasons Keegan stamped his personality all over the club. He was a bundle of dynamite who inspired the Reds to victory after victory at home in England and all across Europe. He and his strike partner, John Toshack, caused mayhem among opposing defenders as they scored goal on goal. In 1972–73 they helped Liverpool win their first Championship in seven years plus their first European trophy, the UEFA Cup. Kevin's workrate was so high that he would be found winning the ball in midfield, running back to his own half to defend and leading the Liverpool attack when going forward. Keegan was the Reds' joint top goalscorer in the League in 1972–73 with 13 goals, and he bagged two in the UEFA Cup final win over Borussia Moenchengladbach. He was already an international, having made his debut for England in their 1–0 win over Wales in Cardiff on 15 November 1972.

In 1974 Liverpool reached the FA Cup final and ironically their third-round opponents were Doncaster Rovers. Keegan scored twice in the 2–2 draw at Anfield before the Reds' won the replay 2–0 (Steve Heighway, Peter Cormack). He scored twice more on the way to Wembley and he also scored two goals in Liverpool's 3–0 win over Newcastle United in the final, Steve Heighway getting the other. The 1974–75 season began badly for Kevin as he was sent off along with Billy Bremner of Leeds United in the FA Charity Shield, and Liverpool finished the season trophyless. Fortunes improved the following season as Keegan won his second League Championship winners' medal and a second UEFA Cup winners' medal, as well as being the 1976 Football Writers' Association Footballer of the Year and England captain.

The 1976–77 season was Keegan's last at Anfield, and he added victory in the European Cup final to a further League Championship title. After 323 appearances and 100 goals, Keegan left Liverpool and joined SV Hamburg for £500,000. In Germany, he twice was named European Footballer of the Year and, when he returned to England, he joined Southampton before becoming a legend at Newcastle United, where he also was manager for two spells.

DID YOU KNOW THAT?
In February 1999, Kevin Keegan became the first former Liverpool player to be appointed England manager.

For the Record

Born: 14 February 1951, Armthorpe, Yorkshire
Country: England, 63 apps, 21 goals
Liverpool appearances: 323
Liverpool goals: 100
Liverpool debut: H v Nottingham Forest,
    14 August 1971, League

Billy Liddell

William "Billy" Liddell was born on 10 January 1922 in Townhill, Dunfermline, Scotland. It was while he was with the Lochgelly Violet club, aged 16 and having turned down a chance to join Hamilton Academicals, that Liddell was persuaded by Liverpool manager George Kay to move south of the border and sign for the Reds. Kay paid Lochgelly Violet £200 for Liddell, who signed for Liverpool as a professional in 1939. However, the start of his career for the Reds was delayed by World War II, during which Liddell served with the RAF in both Britain and Canada. On 5 January 1946, however, the day duly arrived and Liddell made his first-team debut against Chester in the third round of the FA Cup. The game ended 2–2 with Liddell netting a debut goal.

Liddell appeared 34 times for the Liverpool team that lifted the First Division Championship in 1946–47. That season he played alongside future Liverpool manager Bob Paisley, who once said of Liddell: "Billy was so strong, he was unbelievable. From beginning to end he would battle, challenge and show tenacity." It was this fighting spirit that endeared the little Scot to the hearts of the Liverpool fans. However, despite his superhuman performances for the Reds on the pitch, Liverpool inexplicably went downhill after their 1946–47 Championship success.

That First Division Championship winners' medal plus the FA Cup runners-up medal he picked up after the Reds' 1950 FA Cup final defeat to Arsenal seem scant reward for a career which spanned more than 20 years. His career took in over 40 consecutive FA Cup ties and a total of 534 appearances for the Reds in which he scored 228 goals, including one after only 18 seconds in a 3–1 away win over Bristol

City at Ashton Gate on 20 September 1958. Liddell topped the Liverpool goalscoring charts for eight seasons. Billy also played 26 wartime games for the Reds, finding the back of the net 18 times.

Billy Liddell won 28 international caps for Scotland and also made eight "unofficial" international appearances for Scotland during the war. He and Stanley Matthews were the only players selected for the Great Britain representative side in both 1947 and 1955. Liddell's testimonial attracted 38,750 fans, which speaks volumes for the affection in which the Liverpool Scot was held. In August 1960, just a few months before his 40th birthday, Billy Liddell made his final appearance for Liverpool.

Much of his career was played in Division Two, so it was somewhat ironic that, one season after he retired, Liverpool became League champions. Nicknamed "The Flying Scot", he had it all – the strength of an ox and the speed of a gazelle. Billy Liddell died, aged 79, on 3 July 2001.

DID YOU KNOW THAT?

Such was his importance to the Reds that, in the 1950s, the club was nicknamed "Liddellpool".

For the Record

Born: 10 January 1922, Dunfermline, Scotland
Died: 3 July 2001, Mossley Hill, Liverpool
Country: Scotland, 28 apps, 6 goals
Liverpool appearances: 534
Liverpool goals: 228
Liverpool debut: A v Chester, 5 January 1946, FA Cup

Phil Neal

Phil Neal was born on 20 February 1951 in Irchester, Northamptonshire. His football career began with his local Northampton Town, for whom he signed in December 1968. He made his debut for the Cobblers later that season, at the end of which they were relegated to Division Four. At Northampton he was normally played in midfield but was versatile enough to fill other positions when needed. Neal was new Liverpool manager Bob Paisley's first signing, arriving at Anfield for £66,000 in October 1974. He made his debut for the Reds in the Merseyside derby at Goodison Park on 9 October, starting in place of injured left-back Alec Lindsay. He played well in a 0–0 draw in which Terry McDermott also made his Liverpool debut.

Between November 1976 and September 1983 Neal made a record 417 consecutive appearances for the Reds in all competitions before being forced to sit out a European Cup tie against Odense. He was at right-back for the vast majority of these games. During his time at the club, Neal won just about everything there was to win at club level except the FA Cup. His first trophies came in 1975–76 when he won his first League Championship winners' medal and a UEFA Cup winners' medal, and honours gained during the course of his Anfield career include six First Division Championships, four European Cups (the most won by any Liverpool player), one European Super Cup, one UEFA Cup, four League Cups and five FA Charity Shields. Phil's impressive medal collection makes him the most decorated Liverpool player in the club's history.

On 24 March 1976 Don Revie awarded Phil his first England cap in the 2–1 win over Wales in Wrexham. His

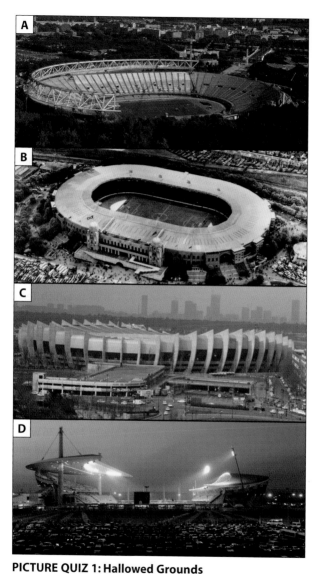

PICTURE QUIZ 1: Hallowed Grounds

Identify these venues for Liverpool's European Cup glory nights. (And at which stadium did they triumph twice?)

PICTURE QUIZ 2: Kop Choir

Which Anfield anthems spring to mind when you peruse these evocative images? Altogether now…

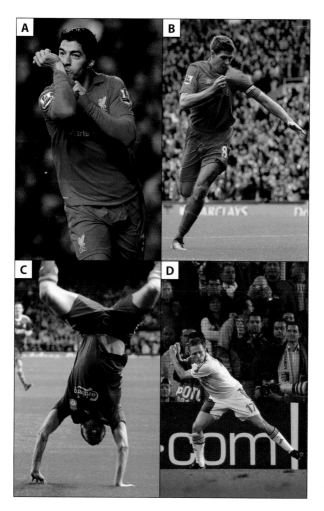

PICTURE QUIZ 3: It's A Celebration

Liverpool players have always known how to put on the style when the goals go in. Can you identify this fantastic foursome?

PICTURE QUIZ 4: The Road to Rio
The following Liverpool players all took part in the 2014
FIFA World Cup qualifying campaign. Who are they? And
name the countries for which they were battling?

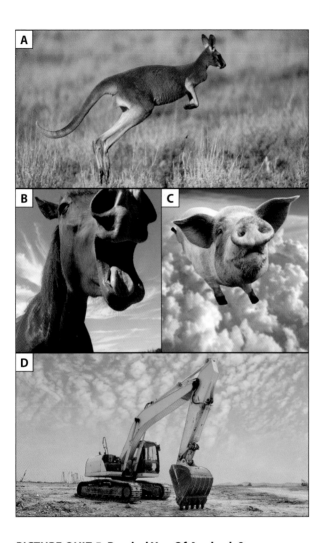

PICTURE QUIZ 5: Remind You Of Anybody?

Anfield has proved fertile ground for player's nicknames.
What's the monicker and who's the player in each case?

PICTURE QUIZ 6: Meet The Gaffer

These four footballers went on to be the manager of the Reds. Can you name them?

PICTURE QUIZ 7: They Shall Not Pass

Liverpool have had many fine goalkeepers down the years. Who are these four esteemed custodians?

PICTURE QUIZ 8: New Kid on the Block

Like the Mounties, these Liverpool managers got their man. Name the new arrivals at Anfield and their proud mentors.

ANSWERS ON PAGE 192

Liverpool team-mates, Clemence, Keegan, Ray Kennedy and Thompson also played. Neal went on to win 50 caps for his country, making his final appearance against Denmark on 21 September 1983, and is the second most capped England right-back of all time.

Neal had an exceptional scoring record at Liverpool, with 59 goals in 650 appearances, albeit most of them coming from the penalty spot. He converted a penalty in the 1977 European Cup final against Borussia Moenchengladbach and was on the mark again against AS Roma in 1984. Phil left Anfield in December 1985 to take up the position of player/manager at Bolton Wanderers. Although he was in charge when the club was relegated to Division Four, he achieved promotion back into Division Three at the first attempt. Neal went on to become boss at Coventry City, Cardiff City and Manchester City and England manager Graham Taylor made Neal his assistant in the early 1990s.

DID YOU KNOW THAT?
Phil Neal was, until passed by Ryan Giggs in 2007, the most successful player in Football League history with eight Championship winners' medals to his name. No English player has won more medals than him.

For the Record

Born: 20 February 1951, Irchester, Northamptonshire
Country: England, 50 apps, 5 goals
Liverpool appearances: 650
Liverpool goals: 59
Liverpool debut: A v Everton, 9 October 1974, League

Bob Paisley, OBE

Robert "Bob" Paisley was born on 23 January 1919 in Hetton-le-Hole, County Durham. He was a member of the Bishop Auckland side that won the FA Amateur Cup in 1939 and joined Liverpool in May that year. World War II delayed his debut for the Reds until 5 January 1946, in which game Liverpool won 2–0 (Liddell, Fagan) away to Chester in the third round of the FA Cup. Paisley went on to make 277 appearances for the Reds, scoring 12 goals. As a player, he won a League champions medal in 1946–47 and received an FA Cup runners-up medal in 1950, although he wasn't in the 11. The FA Cup would prove to be the one major trophy Paisley wouldn't win either as a player or as Liverpool manager. He made his final appearance at the end of the 1953–54 season before joining the Liverpool backroom staff and he became Bill Shankly's assistant in the early 1960s, and a member of the legendary "Boot Room".

When Shankly retired as manager in July 1974, Paisley assumed his mantle as boss. It was the start of the greatest period in Liverpool history. Continuing on from where Shankly had started, Paisley soon achieved even greater glory. In 1976, the Reds won the League Championship and the UEFA Cup. A year later, the title was retained and the Holy Grail of European club football, the European Cup was added to the Liverpool trophy cabinet. Borussia Moenchengladbach were beaten 3–1, with goals from Terry McDermott, Tommy Smith and Phil Neal (a penalty) Only a narrow FA Cup final defeat denied Liverpool the treble.

The success continued in 1978, when a goal from Kenny Dalglish brought Liverpool a second European Cup with a 1–0 defeat of Bruges – losers in the 1976 UEFA Cup final.

After two more League titles in 1979 and 1980, Paisley became the first and, to date, the only manager to win the European Cup for a third time when Liverpool overcame Real Madrid 1–0 (Alan Kennedy) in the final in Paris.

Paisley announced that the 1982–83 season would be his last and defending League champions Liverpool responded by retaining the trophy, his sixth in nine seasons in charge. Another Boot Room boy, Joe Fagan, took over as manager. Bob Paisley died on 14 February 1996. In 2002 he was an Inaugural Inductee of the English Football Hall of Fame in recognition of his contribution to the English game.

DID YOU KNOW THAT?

After he hung up his boots in 1954, Bob Paisley became the club's physiotherapist, though he was self-taught. It was said he could diagnose an injury merely by looking at a player.

For the Record

Born: 23 January 1919, Hetton-le-Hole, County Durham
Died: 14 February 1996, Liverpool

Player (1946–1954)

Liverpool appearances: 277

Liverpool goals: 12

Liverpool debut: A v Chester, 5 January 1946, FA Cup

Manager (1974–1983)

Liverpool record: P490, W275, D91, L124

Liverpool major honours: League Champions (6): 1976, 1977, 1979, 1980, 1982, 1983; European Cup winners (4): 1977, 1978, 1981; UEFA Cup winners (1): 1976; League Cup winners (3): 1981, 1982, 1983

Ian Rush, MBE

Ian Rush was born on 20 October 1961 in St Asaph, Wales. He began his career at Chester, making his debut as a midfielder in April 1979. He became a striker the following season and soon attracted interest from a number of top clubs. In April 1980 Bob Paisley paid Chester £300,000 for the rail-thin, quick teenager, but as it was after the transfer deadline, he couldn't join the Reds until the start of the 1980–81 season.

On 13 December 1980 Rush made his Liverpool debut in a 1–1 (Jimmy Case) draw at Ipswich Town, but he struggled to make an impact that season and grew restless with his lack of first-team opportunities, though he did win a League Cup winners medal after replacing Steve Heighway in the starting line-up for the replayed final against West Ham at Villa Park. Rush approached Paisley, who explained, "You don't score enough goals so you're not worth your place." It was a brutally honest answer and though he contemplated leaving Anfield Rush decided, instead, to dedicate himself to improving his game, especially in front of goal. This new attitude paid immediate dividends as he scored 30 goals in all competitions and won both a first League Championship winner's medal and a second League Cup winner's medal.

Over the course of his Anfield career, spanning two spells with the Reds, club goalscoring records tumbled at his feet. During his first stint with Liverpool, Rush was quite simply the most lethal marksman in British football. He was a goal machine who combined pace with aerial power; he could shoot with both feet, with unerring accuracy and power, and was instinctively in the right place at the right time. Rush scored 346 goals in 660 appearances in his two Liverpool spells – there was a brief interlude with Juventus in 1987–88.

Among his achievements are the twentieth-century career-record of 44 FA Cup goals (39 for Liverpool) and the joint record in the League Cup of 49 goals (shared with Sir Geoff Hurst). He won five First Division Championships, three FA Cups, five League Cups (the first to achieve this feat), one European Cup, four Charity Shields and one Screen Sport Super Cup. Rush also won Europe's Golden Boot Award, was twice Footballer of the Year and received an MBE for services to football.

Wales's record scorer, with 28 goals in 73 appearances, Rush kept his best scoring achievements for Everton. He found the net four times in a 5–0 thrashing of the Toffees at Goodison Park on 6 November 1982 (Mark Lawrenson netted the other) and scored twice in Liverpool's two Merseyside FA Cup final wins, in 1986 and 1989, the latter having come on as a substitute. He wound down his 22-season career with short spells at Leeds United, Newcastle United, Sheffield United, Wrexham and Sydney Olympic in Australia.

DID YOU KNOW THAT?

The £300,000 transfer fee Chester received for Ian Rush in 1980 remained their club record until 2010 when they folded.

For the Record

Born: 20 October 1961, St Asaph, Wales
Country: Wales, 73 apps, 28 goals
Liverpool appearances: 660
Liverpool goals: 346
Liverpool debut: A v Ipswich Town,
  13 December 1980, League

Bill Shankly, OBE

William "Bill" Shankly was born on 2 September 1913 in Glenbuck, an Ayrshire mining village. One of five brothers who all played professional football – he spent most of his career at Preston North End, where he won the FA Cup in 1938 as well as earning five Scottish caps. A brother, Robert, was also a successful manager, guiding Dundee to the Scottish title in 1961–62. Bill moved into management in 1949, taking charge of Carlisle United, Grimsby Town, Workington and Huddersfield Town. After Liverpool, languishing in Division Two, had been knocked out of the FA Cup by Southern League Worcester City in November 1959, Phil Taylor was sacked and Shankly took over as manager in the following month.

He blew through Anfield like a hurricane changing almost everything at the club. He instituted the "Boot Room", where he and his coaches would sit to discuss tactics, changed the club colours to all red, installed the "This is Anfield" sign in the players' tunnel and, most importantly, brought a new attitude to both playing and training. It took a couple of years for things to turn around, but in 1961–62, Liverpool won the Division Two Championship. Two years later, the Football League trophy was back in the Anfield trophy cabinet followed, in 1965, by the FA Cup for the first time in club history.

Shankly's teams were built on a solid, no-nonsense defence with the likes of Ron Yeats and Tommy Smith, a solid midfield containing players such as Peter Thompson, Geoff Strong, Ian Callaghan and Steve Heighway, and lethal strikers, most notably Ian St John, Roger Hunt and Kevin Keegan. From being the second team in Liverpool, the Reds soon became the first team in England. The League

Championship was won in 1966 and again in 1973, when Liverpool – having lost in the European Cup winners' Cup final of 1966 – claimed their first piece of European silverware in the UEFA Cup, beating Borussia Monchengladbach over two legs.

Although Bob Paisley would go on to enjoy even greater success than Shankly at Liverpool, it was the gruff Scotsman's team which he inherited in 1974, following Shankly's shock retirement a few weeks after victory in the FA Cup final. Bill Shankly was awarded the OBE for services to football, and died, aged 68, following a heart attack on 29 September 1981. In 2002 he was made an inaugural inductee of the English Football Hall of Fame, recognising his contribution to the English game as manager of Liverpool.

DID YOU KNOW THAT?
The Shankly Gates were built in memory of the Reds former manager in 1982 and Bill's widow Nessie officially opened them on 26 August 1982. They are a focal point of Anfield.

For the Record

Born: 2 September 1913, Glenbuck, Ayrshire, Scotland
Died: 29 September 1981, Liverpool
Country: Scotland, 5 apps, 0 goals
Manager (1959–1974)
Liverpool record: P783, W407, D198, L178
Liverpool major honours: League Champions (3): 1964, 1966, 1973; FA Cup winners (2): 1965, 1974; UEFA Cup (1): 1973; Division Two Champions (1): 1962; FA Charity Shield (4): 1964 (shared), 1965 (shared), 1966, 1974,

Phil Thompson

Phil Thompson was born on 21 January 1954 in Liverpool and supported Liverpool as a boy, standing on the Kop. He joined the club as a professional on 22 January 1971 from Kirkby Schools and made his debut on 3 April 1972 in a 3–0 (Chris Lawler, John Toshack, Emlyn Hughes) win at Manchester United.

In his first full season at Anfield, 1972–73, Thompson won First Division Championship, UEFA Cup winners' and Reserve Team Championship winners' medals. He soon dislodged centre-back Larry Lloyd, and played at the heart of the Liverpool defence, alongside captain Emlyn Hughes, with Tommy Smith moving to full-back. Phil won an FA Cup winners' medal in 1974, successfully stifling the powerful and prolific Newcastle United striker Malcolm Macdonald at the Wembley showpiece as Liverpool triumphed 3–0 (Kevin Keegan, 2, Steve Heighway). In 1975–76, Thompson was an integral part of the Reds side that lifted the double of League Championship and UEFA Cup.

On 24 March 1976 Don Revie awarded Thompson his first international cap in England's 2–1 win over Wales at Wrexham. He was one of five Anfielders in the team, Ray Clemence, Phil Neal, Kevin Keegan and Ray Kennedy being the others. During the United States Bicentennial Tournament in 1976, he scored his only international goal, in a 3–2 win over Italy in New York. In 1976–77 Phil played enough games to win his third League Championship winners' medal, but missed both the 1977 FA Cup final defeat to Manchester United and the 1977 European Cup victory over Borussia Moenchengladbach through injury. Phil returned to the Liverpool side the following season and won a

European Cup winners' medal in the 1–0 (Kenny Dalglish) win over FC Bruges at Wembley. A year later he won his fourth League Championship winners' medal, and when Emlyn Hughes left Liverpool in August 1979, Bob Paisley made Thompson club captain. Phil's proudest moment as skipper came in the 1981 European Cup final win over Real Madrid in Paris. He later took the trophy to bed and then down to his local pub, The Falcon, in Kirkby, so his mates could have their photographs taken with it.

The Alan Hansen–Mark Lawrenson partnership in defence signalled the end of Thompson's regular place in the Liverpool team and, in 1985, after 477 appearances and 13 goals, he joined Sheffield United. In a glittering career, Thompson won seven League Championships, two European Cups, one FA Cup, two League Cups, six FA Charity Shields, one UEFA Cup and one European Super Cup.

DID YOU KNOW THAT?

A true Red, Phil Thompson returned to Anfield in a coaching capacity. He first worked with Kenny Dalglish, then Gerard Houllier, and when the Frenchman underwent heart surgery late in 2001, Thompson became acting manager.

For the Record

Born: 21 January 1954, Liverpool
Country: England, 42 apps, 1 goal
Liverpool appearances: 477
Liverpool goals: 13
Liverpool debut: A v Manchester United, 3 April 1972, League

CHAPTER

4

LIVERPOOL
FANTASY TEAMS

We've all done it. Sitting in a train or a car with some friends on the way to watch the mighty Reds hand out another beating some hapless opponents. On the way home, we can bask in the glorious memory of the victory and minutely pick through the bones of the match.

But, on the way to the game, what is there to do. Here is one suggestion: why not pick your fantasy Liverpool XI? Or take it a step or two further, pick a selection of Liverpool teams. The possibilities are almost endless; you can choose squads based on the players' names, all As, etc., or maybe all with the same first name.

If you're not sure where to begin, over the next few pages you will find some teams I've devised. The great thing about these fantasy teams is that your choice of players is just as valid as mine. The key word is "fantasy" which means all the players you choose are at the peak of their powers, they never get injured, never miss a sitter or dive over a goalbound shot.

This a really good travel game. All you need is paper and some pens or pencils. Everyone chooses a theme and you have, 20 minutes, to pick your fantasy teams. I've found that if 10 of you play, in almost every case, there will be 10 different fantasy teams chosen. By the way, if you are doing this in a car, please don't ask the driver to write down his or her choices!

Liverpool England XI (pre-1979)

1
Ray
CLEMENCE

2
Phil
NEAL

5
Tommy
SMITH

6
Emlyn
HUGHES
(CAPTAIN)

3
Alec
LINDSAY

6
Ray
KENNEDY

8
Terry
McDERMOTT

11
Ian
CALLAGHAN

7
Kevin
KEEGAN

9
Roger
HUNT

10
Jack
BALMER

Substitutes

Sam *HARDY* · Chris *LAWLER* · Laurie *HUGHES*

Larry *LLOYD* · Alan *A'COURT*

Player-Manager

Kevin *KEEGAN*

DID YOU KNOW THAT?

Kevin Keegan was a key member of England's teams in the 1970s and early 1980s, and captained his country on 31 occasions. However, he played only 27 minutes in World Cup finals. England failed to qualify for both the 1974 and 1978 tournaments, then an injury kept him out of the first round stage in 1982. He did come off the bench after 63 minutes in England's second round group match, against hosts Spain, but the match ended in a goalless draw, so England, like their opponents were knocked out.

Liverpool England X1(1980–2013)

1
David
JAMES

2
Glen
JOHNSON

6
Jamie
CARRAGHER

5
Mark
WRIGHT

3
Alan
KENNEDY

7
Peter
BEARDSLEY

4
Steven
GERRARD
(CAPTAIN)

8
Steve
McMANAMAN

9
Robbie
FOWLER

10
Michael
OWEN

11
John
BARNES

Substitutes

Chris *KIRKLAND* · Raheem *STERLING*

Phil *THOMPSON* · Joe *COLE* · Peter *CROUCH*

Manager

Phil *NEAL*

DID YOU KNOW THAT?

When he played in the 2010 World Cup in South Africa, David James became the oldest player ever to make his first appearance in the finals. He was 39 years and 321 days old.

DID YOU KNOW THAT?

When England beat Germany 5–1 at Munich on 1 September 2001, all the goals came from Liverpool players. Michael Owen bagged a hat-trick and Steve Gerrard and Emile Heskey got the other two.

Liverpool Scottish XI

Substitutes

Bert **SLATER** · Gary **GILLESPIE** · Gary **McALLISTER**

Jimmy **McDOUGALL** · Ian **ST JOHN**

Player-Manager

Matt **BUSBY**

DID YOU KNOW THAT?

Goalkeeper Thomas Younger – who won two Scottish League titles with Hibernian – had to leave the pitch with an injury during a game against Derby County in October 1957, but later returned to play as a centre-forward.

DID YOU KNOW THAT?

Kenny Dalglish was the first player to appear in 100 matches for Scotland. He finished his career with 102 caps and scored 30 goals, a record tally he shares with Denis Law.

Liverpool Irish XI

Substitutes

Jim **BEGLIN** · Kevin **SHEEDY** · Mark **KENNEDY**

Bill **LACEY** · Darren **POTTER**

Player-Manager

Steve **STAUNTON**

DID YOU KNOW THAT?

Legendary goalkeeper Elisha Scott represented Ireland and Northern Ireland. Born in Belfast in 1894, he made his debut for Ireland in 1920, before the Partition. He played five times for Ireland and made 22 appearances for Northern Ireland.

DID YOU KNOW THAT?

Steve Staunton became the first Irishman to make 100 appearances for his country in the 1–1 draw against Germany in the group stages of the 2002 World Cup finals.

Liverpool's European XI

1
Pepe
REINA
(SPAIN)

2
Martin
SKRTEL
(SLOVAKIA)

4
Sami
HYYPIA
(FINLAND)
(CAPTAIN)

5
Stephane
HENCHOZ
(SWITZERLAND)

3
John Arne
RIISE
(NORWAY)

7
Luis
GARCIA
(SPAIN)

6
Jan
MOLBY
(DENMARK)

8
Xabi
ALONSO
(SPAIN)

10
Jari
LITMANEN
(FINLAND)

9
Fernando
TORRES
(SPAIN)

11
Patrik
BERGER
(CZECH REPUBLIC)

Substitutes

Sander **WESTERVELD** *(HOLLAND)* · Stig-Inge **BJORNEBYE** *(NORWAY)*

· Daniel **AGGER** *(DENMARK)* · Dirk **KUYT** *(HOLLAND)* ·

Vladimir **SMICER** *(CZECH REPUBLIC)*

Manager

Gerard **HOULLIER** *(FRANCE)*

DID YOU KNOW THAT?

Xabi Alonso's father, Miguel Angel "Periko" Alonso, played for Barcelona and won two Spanish League winners' medals with Real Sociedad, from whom Liverpool bought Xabi in August 2004.

DID YOU KNOW THAT?

This starting XI won a stunning 60 trophies between them in Liverpool colours – with Jan Molby with 14 of those.

Liverpool World XI

1
Bruce
GROBBELAAR
(ZIMBABWE)

2
Salif
DIAO
(SENEGAL)

6
Avi
COHEN
(ISRAEL)

5
Rigobert
SONG
(CAMEROON)

3
Fabio
AURELIO
(BRAZIL)

10
Momo
SISSOKO
(MALI)

7
Berry
NIEUWENHUYS
(SOUTH AFRICA)

4
Javier
MASCHERANO
(ARGENTINA)

8
Craig
JOHNSTON
(AUSTRALIA)
(CAPTAIN)

9
Gordon
HODGSON
(SOUTH AFRICA)

11
Luis
SUAREZ
(URUGUAY)

Substitutes

Brad **FRIEDEL** *(USA)* · Djimi **TRAORE** *(MALI)* · Robert **PRIDAY** *(SOUTH AFRICA)* ·

Maxi **RODRIGUEZ** *(ARGENTINA)* · Ronny **ROSENTHAL** *(ISRAEL)*

Manager

Roy **HODGSON** *(ENGLAND)*

DID YOU KNOW THAT?

Striker Craig Johnston was born in South Africa to Australian parents, grew up in Australia and considers himself Australian. He did not represent either country, but did play for England at both Under-21 and "B" team levels.

DID YOU KNOW THAT?

Roy Hodgson won the Swedish League Championship with Halmstads BK in 1976 and 1979, a feat he has said was "like turning water into wine".

The all-time Liverpool XI

1
Elisha
SCOTT

2
Phil
NEAL

4
Alan
HANSEN

5
Ron
YEATS

3
Ephraim
LONGWORTH

6
Billy
LIDDELL
(CAPTAIN)

8
Steven
GERRARD

11
Ian
CALLAGHAN

9
Ian
RUSH

10
Robbie
FOWLER

7
Kenny
DALGLISH

Substitutes

Ray **CLEMENCE** · Tommy **SMITH** · Terry **McDERMOTT**
· Michael **OWEN** · Roger **HUNT**

Manager

Bill **SHANKLY**

DID YOU KNOW THAT?

Ian Callaghan was in the England 1966 World Cup squad and made one appearance, the 2–0 group victory over France. The last of his four caps came 11 years later, a 2–0 victory in Luxembourg in the 1978 World Cup qualifying competition.

DID YOU KNOW THAT?

Ephraim Longworth played at full-back more than 370 times for Liverpool and didn't score a single goal, but he did manage one in his five-match England career.

Liverpool Managers XI

1
Matt
McQUEEN
(LIVERPOOL)

2
Phil
NEAL
(BOLTON WANDERERS)

4
Emlyn
HUGHES
(ROTHERHAM UNITED)
(CAPTAIN)

5
Ron
YEATS
(TRANMERE ROVERS)

3
Steve
STAUNTON
(REPUBLIC OF IRELAND)

6
Peter
CORMACK
(PARTICK THISTLE)

8
Graeme
SOUNESS
(LIVERPOOL)

11
John
BARNES
(CELTIC)

7
Kevin
KEEGAN
(NEWCASTLE UNITED)

9
John
TOSHACK
(REAL MADRID)

10
Kenny
DALGLISH
(BLACKBURN ROVERS)

Substitutes

Ian *ST JOHN* *(MOTHERWELL)* • Mark *LAWRENSON* *(PETERBOROUGH UNITED)*

Keith *BURKINSHAW* *(TOTTENHAM HOTSPUR)* • Matt *BUSBY* *(MANCHESTER UNITED)*

John *ALDRIDGE* *(TRANMERE ROVERS)*

Manager

Bob *PAISLEY* *(LIVERPOOL)*

DID YOU KNOW THAT?
John Aldridge joined Tranmere Rovers in 1991 and, in his first season there, equalled the club's goalscoring record of 40. Aldo later managed the club guiding them to the 2000 Worthington Cup final.

DID YOU KNOW THAT?
Steve Staunton's first job in football management was with the Republic of Ireland in 2006.

Liverpool World Cup 2010 XI

1
Pepe
REINA
(SPAIN)

2
Glen
JOHNSON
(ENGLAND)

6
Jamie
CARRAGHER
(ENGLAND)

5
Daniel
AGGER
(DENMARK)

3
Martin
SKRTEL
(SLOVAKIA)

7
Maxi
RODRIGUEZ
(ARGENTINA)

8
Steven
GERRARD
(ENGLAND)
(CAPTAIN)

4
Javier
MASCHERANO
(ARGENTINA)

11
Sotirios
KYRGIAKOS
(GREECE)

9
Fernando
TORRES
(SPAIN)

10
Dirk
KUYT
(HOLLAND)

Substitutes

David ***JAMES*** *(ENGLAND)* · Rigobert ***SONG*** *(CAMEROON)* · Xavi ***ALONSO*** *(SPAIN)*
· Ryan ***BABEL*** *(HOLLAND)* · Peter ***CROUCH*** *(ENGLAND)*

Player-manager

David ***JAMES***

DID YOU KNOW THAT?
The 11 starting players were all at Liverpool in the 2009–10 season, as was Ryan Babel. Neither Babel nor Reina played a single minute of the finals though their teams made it through to the Final, where Spain won 1–0.

DID YOU KNOW THAT?
No FIFA World Cup 2010 managers had any connection with Liverpool, but David James did apply for the Portsmouth job.

Liverpool Premier League XI

1
Pepe
REINA

2
Steve
FINNAN

5
Jamie
CARRAGHER

6
Sami
HYYPIA

3
John Arne
RIISE

4
Xabi
ALONSO

8
Steven
GERRARD
(CAPTAIN)

11
John
BARNES

7
Luis
SUAREZ

9
Ian
RUSH

10
Robbie
FOWLER

Substitutes

David **JAMES** · Mark **WRIGHT** · Javier **MASCHERANO**

Michael **OWEN** · Fernando **TORRES**

Manager

Gerard **HOULLIER**

DID YOU KNOW THAT?

Four of the "starting XI" were born either in Liverpool itself or within a few miles of the city: Jamie Carragher, Steven Gerrard, Steve McManaman and Robbie Fowler.

DID YOU KNOW THAT?

With 573 appearances, goalkeeper David James leads the all-time Premier League chart. His chances of adding to that total disappeared when he signed for Championship club Bristol City, after playing for England at the World Cup in 2010.

CHAPTER

5

UP FOR THE CUP

Strange as it may seem to many Liverpool fans, cup success and Anfield were mutually exclusive topics for more than 70 years. The Reds may have won half a dozen League Championships, but there was no FA Cup, League Cup or anything from Europe in the Anfield trophy cabinet until 1965. In fact, Liverpool played in only two finals before the arrival of Bill Shankly: in 1914, against Burnley, and 1950, when Arsenal triumphed.

Since then, it has been a very different matter. In the 47 years since 1965, the FA Cup has come to Anfield on seven occasions, the League Cup eight times, then there are the five European Cups, three UEFA Cups, numerous FA Charity Shields and UEFA Super Cups.

This section concentrates only on England's two major cup competitions, the FA Cup and Football League Cup. All 15 triumphs are chronicled here, with a brief report, a review of the Reds' path to the final together with full match details, date, venue, score, attendance, goalscorers and Liverpool line-ups (including subs). There is also a brief look at the 11 days when things didn't go Liverpool's way,

As the 2011–12 season drifts into the memory, we can always look back on those great afternoons and evenings when the captain strode forward, picked up the cup and raised it towards to the cheering Liverpool fans. "Ee-aye addio, we won the cup!"

1964–65 FA Cup

Liverpool finally got their hands on the FA Cup in their third final. Bill Shankly's men beat West Bromwich Albion 2–1 away in round three, needed replays to see off Stockport County in the fourth round and Leicester City in the quarter-final. In between, Bolton Wanderers were despatched 1–0 at Burnden Park thanks to an Ian Callaghan goal. Liverpool eased past Chelsea 2–0 at Villa Park in the semi-final, to set up a meeting with Leeds United, managed by Don Revie, in their first final. These rivals would be two of the most dominant English teams of the next decade, both having just climbed out of Division Two. The Reds suffered a blow when left-back Gerry Byrne broke his collarbone and, in the days before substitutes, he had to play on. And it was his cross, three minutes into extra time which saw the deadlock broken, Roger Hunt scoring. Seven minutes later, Billy Bremner equalised, but after 113 minutes, Ian St John headed home a Callaghan cross to bring the Cup to Anfield for the first time.

FA CUP FINAL

1 MAY 1965, WEMBLEY STADIUM, Att. 100,000

Liverpool (0) **2**   v   **Leeds United** (0) **1**

Hunt, St John   Bremner

After extra time

Liverpool: Lawrence, Lawler, Byrne, Strong, Yeats, Stevenson,

Callaghan, Hunt, St John, Smith, Thompson

DID YOU KNOW THAT?

The 1965 FA Cup final was the first one for 18 years to require extra-time. Since then, the longest gap between finals going to extra time is 12 years, 1993–2005

1973–74 FA Cup

To win the FA Cup for the second time in club history, Liverpool made heavy weather of reaching the latter stages, but were then almost irresistible. Replays were needed for the Reds to advance against Doncaster Rovers and Carlisle United in rounds three and four, but Ipswich Town and Bristol City were brushed aside as Liverpool faced a semi-final date with Leicester City at Old Trafford. The first game ended goalless, and Liverpool won the replay 3–1 (Brian Hall, Kevin Keegan, John Toshack) at Villa Park to reach their sixth final. Newcastle had similar struggles before reaching the final, and needed replays to see off Hendon, Scunthorpe United and Nottingham Forest. Their attack was led the prolific Malcolm MacDonald, but in the final he was kept quiet by Phil Thompson and Emlyn Hughes. The Magpies, however, could not do the same to Liverpool and the only surprise was that it took 57 minutes for the Reds to score, Keegan doing the honours. Steve Heighway added a second goal and Keegan finished the rout two minutes from time.

FA CUP FINAL

4 MAY 1974, WEMBLEY STADIUM, Att. 100,000

Liverpool (0) **3** v **Newcastle United** (0) **0**

Keegan (2), Heighway

Liverpool: Clemence, Smith, Lindsay, P. Thompson, Cormack, Hughes, Keegan, Hall, Heighway , Toshack, Callaghan

DID YOU KNOW THAT?
Two members of the Newcastle team which lost to Liverpool would enjoy long careers at Anfield, scoring in European Cup finals: Terry McDermott (1977) and Alan Kennedy (1984).

1980–81 Football League Cup

It was a source of some amazement that, for all of their domination at home and abroad, Liverpool had never won the Football League Cup. That changed in 1980–81 as the Reds won the trophy for the first time. Bradford City, Swindon Town, Portsmouth and Birmingham City were seen off before Manchester City succumbed 2–1 on aggregate in the semi-final. In the final, Ray Stewart scored an extra-time penalty to put West Ham United on the brink of glory at Wembley, but Alan Kennedy equalised in the 118th minute to force a replay. On 1 April 1981, in the replay at Villa Park, Liverpool made no mistake and finally got their hands on the League Cup. All the goals came inside the first 30 minutes, Paul Goddard giving the Hammers the lead, but Kenny Dalglish equalised after 25 minutes and Alan Hansen got what proved to be the winner three minutes later.

LEAGUE CUP FINAL

14 MARCH 1981, WEMBLEY, ATT. 100,000

Liverpool (0) **1**   **v**   **West Ham United** (0) **1**

A. Kennedy   Stewart (pen)

After extra time

Liverpool: Clemence, Neal, A. Kennedy, Hansen, Irwin,

R. Kennedy, McDermott, Souness, Lee, Dalglish, Heighway (Case)

REPLAY

1 APRIL 1981, VILLA PARK, BIRMINGHAM, ATT. 36,693

Liverpool (2) **2**   **v**   **West Ham United** (1) **1**

Dalglish, Hansen   Goddard

Liverpool: Clemence, Neal, A. Kennedy, Hansen, Thompson, R. Kennedy,

McDermott, Lee, Souness, Dalglish, Rush

1981–82 Football League Cup

There is a saying about waiting for a bus, that you wait ages for one and then two come together. It was like that with Liverpool and the League Cup because, in 1982, they retained the trophy they had won for the first time a year earlier. The Reds crushed Exeter City 11–0 on aggregate before beating Middlesbrough in round three. Both Arsenal and Barnsley battled to replays before they were seen off. Liverpool booked their return to Wembley by defeating Ipswich Town 4–2 on aggregate in the semi-final. The final pitted the 1981 League Cup and FA Cup winners, Liverpool and Tottenham Hotspur and it was a close affair. Steve Archibald gave Spurs the lead after 11 minutes and they held it until the 87th minute, when Ronnie Whelan scored to force extra-time. Liverpool proved the fitter in the extra 30 minutes and won the Cup with goals from Whelan, again, and Ian Rush, both coming in the last 10 minutes.

MILK CUP FINAL

13 MARCH 1982, WEMBLEY STADIUM, Att. 100,000

Liverpool (0) **3**   v   **Tottenham Hotspur** (1)**1**

Whelan 2, Rush   Archibald

After extra time

Liverpool: Grobbelaar, Neal, A. Kennedy, Lawrenson, Thompson, Johnston, Lee, McDermott (Johnson), Souness, Dalglish, Rush

DID YOU KNOW THAT?

Sponsorship of English football began as recently as the mid-1970s and the first major competition to be sponsored was the 1981–82 Football League Cup. With the backing of the Milk Marketing Board, it was renamed the Milk Cup.

1982–83 Football League Cup

In 1982–83 Liverpool won their third consecutive League Cup, beating Manchester United 2–1 after extra time in the final at Wembley. Liverpool began with a 4–1 aggregate win over Ipswich Town in round two, then beat Rotherham United, 1–0, Norwich City, 2–0, and West Ham United, 2–1, in the next three rounds, all at Anfield. Burnley were beaten 3–1 over two legs in the semi-finals to set up a repeat of the 1977 FA Cup Final. Norman Whiteside gave United the lead at Wembley, only for Alan Kennedy – a regular finals goalscorer – to send the game into extra time with his 75th minute equaliser. After 98 minutes, the 1982 League Cup final match-winner Ronnie Whelan repeated the feat, as Liverpool avenged their defeat six years earlier.

MILK CUP FINAL
26 MARCH 1983, WEMBLEY STADIUM, Att. 100,000
Liverpool (0) **2**   vs   **Manchester United** (1) **1**
A. Kennedy, Whelan   Whiteside
After extra time

Liverpool: Grobbelaar, Neal, A. Kennedy, Hansen, Lawrenson, Whelan, Johnston

(Fairclough), Lee, Souness, Dalglish, Rush

DID YOU KNOW THAT?
For the three years in a row, the team Liverpool beat in the League Cup final would go on to win that season's FA Cup. Spurs retained their FA Cup in 1982, Manchester United won it in 1983, and Everton took the trophy in 1984. Liverpool's first League Cup final victims, West Ham United in 1981, had won the FA Cup a year earlier.

1983–84 Football League Cup

Liverpool were made to work exceptionally hard to win their fourth consecutive Football League Cup. After a comfortable 8–1 aggregate win over Brentford in round two, Fulham were only seen off in a second round second replay. Birmingham City were then downed 3–0 at the second attempt at Anfield, as were Sheffield Wednesday. Walsall held the Reds to a first leg 2–2 draw at Anfield before they lost the semi-final second leg 2–0 at Fellows Park. It was a Mersey derby in the 1984 Milk Cup final and the match Wembley ended goalless after 120 minutes. In the replay at Maine Road, Manchester, Graeme Souness scored the only goal to win the cup for Liverpool.

MILK CUP FINAL

25 MARCH 1984, WEMBLEY STADIUM, ATT. 100,000

Liverpool (0) **0**   vs   **Everton** (0) **0**

After extra time

Liverpool: Grobbelaar, Neal, A. Kennedy, Lawrenson, Hansen, Whelan, Lee, Johnston (Robinson), Souness, Dalglish, Rush

REPLAY

28 MARCH 1984, MAINE ROAD, MANCHESTER, ATT. 52,089

Liverpool (1) **1**   vs   **Everton** (0) **0**

Souness

Liverpool: Grobbelaar, Neal, A. Kennedy, Lawrenson, Hansen, Whelan, Souness, Lee, Johnston, Rush, Dalglish

DID YOU KNOW THAT?

Liverpool played a record 13 games on their way to winning six 1983–84 League Cup rounds. They met five opponents twice – two in two-legged ties – and Fulham three times.

1985–86 FA Cup

Two years after meeting in the Milk Cup final, a Merseyside derby decided the 1986 FA Cup and, again, Liverpool won it. To reach the final, Liverpool beat Norwich City, Chelsea, York City (surprisinginly only after a replay), Watford (again at the second attempt following a draw at Anfield) and Southampton, who went down 2–0 at White Hart Lane in the semi-final. In the first Merseyside FA Cup , Gary Lineker gave the Toffees the lead only five minutes but Liverpool stormed back to claim their third FA Cup success. Ian Rush equalised after 56 minutes, Craig Johnston made it 2–1 seven minutes later, and Rush finished off Liverpool's victory after 83 minutes as the Reds completed the Double.

FA CUP FINAL

10 MAY 1986, WEMBLEY STADIUM, ATT. 98,000

Liverpool (0) **3**   v   **Everton** (0) **1**

Rush (2), Johnston   Lineker

Liverpool: Grobbelaar, Beglin, Nicol, Lawrenson, Hansen, Molby, Whelan, Johnston, MacDonald, Rush, Dalglish

DID YOU KNOW THAT?

Republic of Ireland star Mark Lawrenson, born near Preston, was the only English born player in Liverpool's starting 11 (Steve McMahon was the substitute). The Reds thus became the first FA Cup final team without a single England player.

DID YOU KNOW THAT?

Only two of Liverpool's squad in the final were not full internationals: Kevin MacDonald (a Scotsman) and Craig Johnston (an Australian, but born in South Africa)

1988–89 FA Cup

Liverpool's fourth FA Cup success will for ever be overshadowed by the Hillsborough Disaster on 15 April 1989, when 96 Liverpool fans died attending the semi-final against Nottingham Forest in Sheffield. The Reds recorded away wins in their first three ties, at Carlisle United, Millwall and Hull City 3–2 before easily disposing of Brentford at Anfield in the quarter-final. Then came the semi-final against Nottingham Forest at Hillsborough. The match was suspended after six minutes, then abandoned, as the tragedy grew. The match was replayed on 7 May, at Old Trafford, where Liverpool won 3–1 (John Aldridge, 2, Brian Laws own goal). In the final, delayed by the tragedy until 20 May, Everton were the opponents and, on an emotional afternoon at Wembley, Gerry Marsden led a rendition of "You'll Never Walk Alone" before the kick-off. Aldridge's goal seemed to have won the game, until Stuart McCall equalised at the death. In extra time, Ian Rush scored twice, either side of another McCall strike, to give Liverpool the trophy.

FA CUP FINAL

20 MAY 1989, WEMBLEY STADIUM, ATT. 82,500

Liverpool (1) **3**　　**v**　　**Everton** (0) **2**

Aldridge, Rush (2)　　　　　　McCall (2)

After extra time

Liverpool: Grobbelaar, Ablett, Staunton (Venison), Nicol, Hansen, Whelan, Houghton, Barnes, McMahon, Beardsley, Aldridge (Rush)

DID YOU KNOW THAT?

For the first time in an FA Cup final, both teams got two goals from one of their substitutes: Ian Rush and Stuart McCall.

1991–92 FA Cup

Ian Rush was the star, and scorer of the second goal, as Liverpool beat Second Division Sunderland 2–0 to win the 1992 FA Cup final at Wembley. It was another tough battle for the Reds, once they had seen off the challenge of Crewe Alexandra at Gresty Road 4–0 in the third round. Liverpool travelled to Bristol Rovers in round four and only advanced after winning 2–1 at Anfield in a replay. Another Anfield replay was needed in the last 16, as Ipswich Town held the Reds to a goalless draw at Portman Road before falling 3–2. A 1–0 win over Aston Villa in the sixth round earned the Reds a semi-final tie against Portsmouth. Again, it took two games to see off the south coast side and this time the replay was only decided by a penalty shoot-out, Liverpool reaching Wembley 3–1. Sunderland were outplayed by the Reds and striker John Byrne – looking to score in every round of the competition – barely had a look in, though he did miss one great chance. Michael Thomas scored early in the second half to give Graeme Souness's men the lead and Rush got the second midway through the half.

FA CUP FINAL
9 MAY 1992, WEMBLEY, ATT. 79,544

Liverpool (0) **2**　　v　　**Sunderland** (0) **0**

Thomas, Rush

Liverpool: Grobbelaar, Jones, Burrows, Nicol, Wright, Houghton, Molby,

McManaman, Thomas, Rush, Saunders

DID YOU KNOW THAT?
None of the players in the 1992 FA Cup final were still with their respective teams at the end of the century

1994–95 Football League Cup

In 1995 Liverpool won the Coca-Cola Cup (League Cup) with a 2–1 win over Bolton Wanderers in the final at Wembley. On their way to their fifth success in the competition, Liverpool started with a 6–1 aggregate win over Burnley in round two. In the third round the Reds saw off Stoke City 2–1 at Anfield and followed this up with a 3–1 away victory over Kenny Dalglish's Blackburn Rovers. An Ian Rush goal ended Arsenal's quarter-final challenge at Anfield, while Robbie Fowler scored the only goal in both legs of the semi-final tie against Crystal Palace. Bolton were making their first appearance at a Wembley final since the FA Cup in 1958 and they struggled to contain Steve McManaman, who dominated the match. He scored the opening goal eight minutes before half-time and doubled Liverpool's lead after 68 minutes. Although Alan Thompson pulled a goal back almost immediately, Liverpool were able to take the trophy back to Anfield.

COCA COLA CUP FINAL

2 APRIL 1995, WEMBLEY, ATT. 75,595

Liverpool (1) **2**	**v**	**Bolton Wanderers** (0) **1**
McManaman 2		Thompson

Liverpool: James, Jones, Bjornebye, Scales, Ruddock, Babb, McManaman, Redknapp, Barnes, Rush, Fowler

DID YOU KNOW THAT?
The 1995 League Cup final referee, Philip Don, had been in charge of Liverpool's previous Wembley cup final victory, the 1992 FA Cup against Sunderland. No referee has officiated in two FA Cup finals (excluding replays) since 1901.

2000–01 Football League Cup

In 2001 Liverpool won the first League Cup final to be held at the Millennium Stadium, Cardiff. Liverpool began their 2000–01 Worthington Cup campaign with a 2–1 extra-time home win over Chelsea in the third round. Stoke City were then hammered 8–0 at the Britannia Stadium, before three extra time goals at Anfield ended Fulham's challenge. Another London team, Crystal Palace, were Liverpool's semi-final opponents. Liverpool lost the first leg 2–1 at Selhurst Park but responded with a 5–0 thumping at Anfield in the return. In the final Liverpool met a tenacious Birmingham City side, who trailed to a Robbie Fowler goal after half an hour. A stoppage time penalty from Darren Purse brought extra time, then, after a goalless 30 minutes, a penalty shoot-out. Liverpool held their nerve and lifted their sixth League Cup, winning 5–4 in the shoot-out, with Gary McAllister, Nicky Barmby, Christian Ziege, Fowler and, decisively, Jamie Carragher all scoring with their attempts.

WORTHINGTON CUP FINAL

25 FEBRUARY 2001, MILLENNIUM STADIUM, CARDIFF, ATT. 73,500

Liverpool (1) **1**   v   **Birmingham City** (0) **1**

Fowler   Purse (pen)

Liverpool won 5–4 on penalties after extra time

Liverpool: Westerveld, Carragher, Hyppia, Henchoz, Babbel, Hamman, Smicer (Barmby), Gerrard (McAllister), Biscan (Ziege), Heskey, Fowler

DID YOU KNOW THAT?
Liverpool's 8–0 demolition of Stoke City in the fourth round of the Worthington Cup remains the Potteries club's worst ever home defeat.

2000–01 FA Cup

Three months after lifting the Worthington Cup, Liverpool returned to the Millennium Stadium for the FA Cup final. To get to Cardiff, Liverpool had beaten Rotherham United, Leeds United, Manchester City and Tranmere Rovers, before ending the fairy-tale run of Wycombe Wanderers in the semi-final at Villa Park. This was the third time Liverpool had faced Arsenal in an FA Cup final and the Gunners had won the first two (in 1950 and 1971, both at Wembley). It seemed that the script was going to be the same as before, especially when Freddie Ljungberg scored for Arsenal with just 18 minutes remaining. But Gerrard Houllier's team had gained a reputation for never giving up and when Patrik Berger and Robbie Fowler replaced Vladimir Smicer and Danny Murphy, the Reds had four forwards on the pitch, joining Michael Owen, Emile Heskey, plus Steve Gerrard. They needed only Owen, however, and he scored twice in the last seven minutes to break Arsenal's hearts.

FA CUP FINAL

12 MAY 2001, MILLENNIUM STADIUM, CARDIFF, ATT. 74,200

Liverpool (0) **2**   **v**   **Arsenal** (0) **1**

Owen (2)   Ljungberg

Liverpool: Westerveld, Babbel, Hyypia, Henchoz, Carragher, Hamann (McAllister), Murphy (Berger), Smicer (Fowler), Gerrard, Owen, Heskey

DID YOU KNOW THAT?

Liverpool were the first club in eight seasons to achieve the double of the FA Cup and Football League Cup in the same season. Amazingly, when Arsenal did it in 1993, they defeated the same opponents, Sheffield Wednesday, in both finals.

2002–03 Football League Cup

Liverpool won the League Cup for the seventh time with a 2–0 victory over Manchester United in the 2003 Worthington Cup final at the Millennium Stadium, Cardiff. The Reds overcame Southampton in round three, before winning a penalty shoot-out against Ipswich Town and edging past Aston Villa 4–3 in a thrilling quarter-final at Villa Park. It wasn't plain sailing in the semi-final against Sheffield United, with Liverpool edging it 3–2 on aggregate. Liverpool's victory over United in Cardiff was their second against them in a League Cup final (they had won in 1983). Two of England's top internationals provided the goals, the outstanding Steven Gerrard, with a deflection off David Beckham after 39 minutes, and Michael Owen late on.

WORTHINGTON CUP FINAL

2 MARCH 2003, MILLENNIUM STADIUM, CARDIFF, Att. 74,500

Liverpool (1) **2**   v   **Manchester United** (0) **0**

Gerrard, Owen

Liverpool: Dudek, Carragher, Henchoz, Hyypia, Riise, Diouf (Biscan), Hamann, Gerrard, Murphy, Owen, Heskey (Baros [Smicer])

DID YOU KNOW THAT?

All 26 players who appeared in the final were internationals. Pegguy Arphexhad, Liverpool's second goalkeeper, was the only player of the 32 in the two squads not to gain a full cap.

DID YOU KNOW THAT?

Milan Baros played only 28 minutes. He came on as a 61st minute substitute, for Emile Heskey, and was replaced by Vladimir Smicer in the penultimate minute.

2005–06 FA Cup

Liverpool won the 2006 FA Cup final after a nail-biting penalty shoot-out, just as they had in the Champions League final in Istanbul a year earlier. On the road to Cardff, Rafa Benitez's men disposed of Luton Town, Portsmouth, Manchester United and Birmingham City before a semi-final clash against Chelsea at Old Trafford, which Liverpool won 2–1. The last FA Cup final at the Millennium Stadium was also one of the best ever. West Ham United, in their first FA Cup Final in 26 years, led 2–0, thanks to Jamie Carragher (own goal) and Dean Ashton. The Reds fought back with goals from Djibril Cisse and Steven Gerrard. Paul Konchesky's cross-cum-shot restored the Hammers' lead midway through the second half but, in stoppage time, Gerrard, lashed a 30-yard drive past Shaka Hislop to force extra time. The additional 30 minutes produced no goals, and Pepe Reina became Liverpool's hero with three saves in the shoot-out to give Liverpool their seventh FA Cup.

FA CUP FINAL

13 MAY 2006, MILLENNIUM STADIUM, CARDIFF, Att. 71,140

Liverpool (1) **3**	**v**	**West Ham United** (2) **3**
Cisse, Gerrard 2		Carragher (o.g.), Ashton, Konchesky

Liverpool won 3–1 on penalties after extra time

Liverpool: Reina, Finnan, Hyypia, Carragher, Riise, Kewell (Morientes), Gerrard, Sissoko, Alonso (Kromkamp), Cisse, Crouch (Hamman)

DID YOU KNOW THAT?

Spanish international goalkeeper Pepe Reina had a great reputation as a penalty-saver with his former club Villareal.

2011–12 Football League Cup

Liverpool won the League Cup for the eighth time beating Cardiff City on penalties in the 2012 final at Wembley. The Reds were drawn away in every round, but won at Exeter City, Brighton & Hove Albion, Stoke City and Chelsea, before champions-to-be Manchester City were seen off in the two-legged semi-final – the Reds again winning the away leg. Cardiff provided the opposition in the final and it was the Welsh club which took the lead through Joe Mason after 19 minutes. Martin Skrtel headed the equaliser from a corner after an hour, but that was the last goal of the 90 minutes. Manager Kenny Dalglish sent on Dirk Kuyt after 103 minutes and, five minutes later, he gave the Reds the lead. However, with two minutes of extra time remaining, Ben Turner levelled matters for Cardiff to set up a penalty shoot-out. Only one of the first five kicks were converted, by Cardiff's Don Cowie, but then Kuyt, Stewart Downing and Glen Johnson made no mistake, while Anthony Gerrard crucially missed for Cardiff.

CARLING CUP FINAL
26 FEBRUARY 2012, WEMBLEY, Att. 74,500

Liverpool (0) **2** v **Cardiff City** (1) **2**

Skrtel, Kuyt Mason, Turner

Liverpool won 3–2 on penalties after extra time

Liverpool: Reina, Johnson, Enrique, Agger (Carragher), Skrtel, Gerrard, Henderson (Bellamy), Downing, Adam, Suarez, Carroll (Kuyt)

DID YOU KNOW THAT?
Steven Gerrard had the rare experience of playing against his cousin, Anthony Gerrard, in the final and, amazingly, both failed to score with their attempts in the penalty shoot-out.

The ones that got away

As well as their seven FA Cup final victories and eight successes in the Football League Cup, Liverpool have been beaten in seven FA Cup finals and three times in the League Cup. These were the days when things didn't go quite right:

FA CUP FINAL
25 APRIL 1914, CRYSTAL PALACE
Burnley 1 (Freeman), **Liverpool 0**

29 APRIL 1950, WEMBLEY
Arsenal 2 (Lewis 2), **Liverpool 0**

8 MAY 1971, WEMBLEY
Arsenal 2 (Kelly, George), **Liverpool 1** (Heighway), *aet*

21 MAY 1977, WEMBLEY
Manchester Utd 2 (Pearson, J. Greenhoff), **Liverpool 1** (Case)

14 MAY 1988, WEMBLEY
Wimbledon 1 (Sanchez), **Liverpool 0**

11 MAY 1996, WEMBLEY
Manchester United 1 (Cantona), **Liverpool 0**

5 MAY 2012, WEMBLEY
Chelsea 2 (Ramires, Drogba), **Liverpool 1** (Carroll)

FOOTBALL LEAGUE CUP FINAL
18 MARCH 1978, WEMBLEY
Nottingham Forest 0, Liverpool 0, *aet*
22 MARCH 1978, OLD TRAFFORD (REPLAY)
Nottingham Forest 1 (Robertson), **Liverpool 0**

5 APRIL 1987, WEMBLEY
Arsenal 2 (Nicholas 2), **Liverpool 1** (Rush)

27 FEBRUARY 2005, CARDIFF
Chelsea 3 (Gerrard o.g., Drogba, Kezman)
Liverpool 2 (Riise, Nunez), *aet*

CHAPTER

6

WHAT THE REDS SAID

A wise man once said, "Football is all about opinions."
He must have been a Liverpool fan, judging by the
breathtaking range of subjects upon which Reds fans
are are acknowledge experts.

There is no football manager in the history of
the game who has been quoted more often than
the Anfield legend himself, Bill Shankly. I easily could
have devoted this entire chapter to the pearls of
wisdom which emanated from the lips of genius
from Glenbuck, but then I would have missed some
other gems from other Liverpool greats, and he did
retire some 37 years ago.

Each page focuses on a different Liverpool topic,
whether it is what makes the club tick, what it means
to wear the Red shirt and play at Anfield, or to be an
opponent. Some are short and sweet, to the point of
pithy, others more considered; many were uttered
by players and managers moments after incredible
results, a few said reflectively when the immediate
moment has passed.

You probably have your own favourite Liverpool
quote and, hopefully, it is in here. As you read through
our selection, why don't you come up with your own
list? You can make it another travel game. Choose a
topic, or an individual and see if you can come up
with five or ten quotes. Once more, unlike a quiz,
there are no wrong answers, so you can't win or lose.

The Liverpool Way

1

"When you have a Liverpool shirt on your back as part of the squad, you will do anything to make sure you preserve what it stands for"

Gerard Houllier

2

"Liverpool Football Club is all about winning things and being a source of pride to our fans. It has no other purpose."

David Moores, *former Liverpool FC chairman*

3

"It's not about the long ball or the short ball; it's about the right ball."

Bob Paisley

4

"If I told people that the secret of Liverpool's success is a dip in the Mersey three times a week, I not only reckon they'd believe me but I think our river would be full of footballers from all over the country."

Ronnie Moran

5

"The Liverpool philosophy is simple, and it is based on total belief. Maybe that has been the key to Liverpool's consistency. We were taught to go out there, play our own game and fear no one."

Phil Neal

Bill Shankly

1

"Shankly gave the players and the city their pride and passion back. If you didn't have the pride and the passion, then you didn't play for Shankly and you didn't play for Liverpool."

Ricky Tomlinson, *comedian and Liverpool fan*

2

"In my time at Anfield we always said we had the best two teams on Merseyside – Liverpool and Liverpool Reserves."

Bill Shankly

3

"He was a great man. His motivation could move mountains."

Ron Yeats *pays tribute to Shankly*

4

"Take that poof bandage off, and what do you mean you've hurt your knee? It's Liverpool's knee!."

Shankly, *to an injured Tommy Smith*

5

"I want to build a team that's invincible, so they'll have to send a team from Mars to beat us."

Shankly

Anfield arrivals

1

"Some friends asked: 'Why are you moving to Liverpool when you play for Bayern Munich?' Now they realise it was a great opportunity."

Markus Babbel

2

"From my first day at Melwood, I appreciated Liverpool's special DNA."

John Barnes

3

"He's just stepped out of the shower. Come in and see him … have a walk round him. He's a colossus."

Bill Shankly, *unveiling new signing Ron Yeats*

4

"He is the best player that Liverpool have signed this century. It was the best decision we have ever made. He sets such a fine example, not just to our players but to everybody in the game."

John Smith, *Liverpool chairman on signing Kenny Dalglish in 1977*

5

"Kenny Dalglish was the reason I signed for Liverpool. It was his reputation and his stature in the game that persuaded me, and the fact that he gave me a particularly smart pair of boots. It is the only 'bung' I received. They were two sizes too big for me, but I didn't half look good in them."

Steve McManaman

Euro glory nights

1

"I was really confident. I took a penalty in training and put it in the same spot. Just like that."

Alan Kennedy, *on his European Cup final winning penalty against AS Roma, 1984*

2

"The day after we won our first European Cup, we were back at this club at 9.45 in the morning, talking about how we would do it again, working from that moment, because nobody has the right to win anything they haven't earned."

Bob Paisley

3

"I think the game will be a dull 0–0."

Johan Cruyff, *previewing the 2001 UEFA Cup Final against Alaves, which Liverpool won 5–4*

4

"I'm on top of the world. This is the best night of my life."

Steven Gerrard, *on winning the 2005 UEFA Champions League final*

5

"Carra came up to me like he was crazy. He grabbed me and said, 'Jerzy, Jerzy, Jerzy – remember Bruce [Grobbelaar]? He did crazy things in 1984. You have to do the same.' He told me I would be the hero."

Jerzy Dudek, *describing his 'starfish with jelly legs' routine in the 2005 UEFA Champions League Final penalty shoot-out*

Liverpool legends

1

"I never saw anyone in this country to touch him. I can think of only two who could go ahead of him – Pelé and possibly Cruyff."

Graeme Souness, *on Kenny Dalglish*

2

"Keegan had a Doncaster childhood and a Scunthorpe upbringing, yet he seems to have been born with Liverpool in his soul."

Joe Mercer, *former Manchester City and England caretaker manager*

3

"Bob would call us together on a Friday morning and usually just say, 'The same team as last week', and we would get on with it."

Mark Lawrenson, *talking about Bob Paisley*

4

"Tommy Smith wasn't born, he was quarried."

David Coleman, *former BBC Television football commentator'*

5

"I thought it was a bit cruel of Liverpool to put Steven Gerrard on when we were getting tired!."

Ken McKenna, *manager of Welsh League club Total Network Solutions when the skipper was brought on late in a UEFA Champions League qualifier, 2005*

Anfield

1

"Every time I come to this place (Anfield) I think, 'This is brilliant, I'm playing for Liverpool.'"

Nick Barmby

2

"The Kop's exclusive, an institution, and if you're a member of the Kop you feel you're a member of a society, you've got thousands of friends around you."

Bill Shankly

3

"That first night was the greatest. We were in the front row of the Kemlyn stand. The whole time my eyes were fixed on the Kop. I couldn't believe it. I was mesmerised. The steam was rising and the noise was incredible."

Phil Thompson, *recalling his first visit to Anfield at the age of 11*

4

"You had to be strong to be on the Kop. When I was about 13, I tried to go in the middle where all the excitement was and almost got cut in half. I was only 5ft 7in. A big docker pushed the crowd back and I ducked out and went back to my usual place to the left of the goal."

Elvis Costello

5

"It's there to remind our lads who they're playing for, and to remind the opposition who they're playing against."

Bill Shankly, *on the "This is Anfield" sign in the players' tunnel*

The lighter side

1

"There are two great teams in Liverpool: Liverpool and Liverpool Reserves."
Bill Shankly

2

"Mind you, I've been here during the bad times too. One year we came second."
Bob Paisley

3

"If he stays out of night clubs for the next few years, he can buy one."
Gerard Houllier, *on the potential of Steven Gerrard*

4

"The White Pelé? You're more like the White Nellie!"
Bill Shankly, *criticising winger Peter Thompson after he had starred for England but struggled at Anfield*

5

"Tommy Smith would start a riot in a graveyard."
Bill Shankly

The Everton rivalry

1

"If Everton were playing at the bottom of my garden, I'd draw the curtains."

Bill Shankly

2

"Don't worry, Alan. You'll be playing near a great side."

Shankly, *to Alan Ball after he decided to sign for Everton in 1966*

3

"Are we talking about a change of religion here or just a change of football club?"

Gerard Houllier, *on the furore surrounding Nick Barmby's move across Stanley Park*

4

"We gave four great examples of how to score goals, and four bad examples of how to defend."

Kenny Dalglish, *after the 4–4 FA Cup draw with Everton in 1991*

5

""Tell ya ma, ya ma,
To wipe away all your tears,
No trophies for 15 years,
Tell ya ma, ya ma."

Liverpool fans chant, *after the 2009–10 Derby at Goodison had ended 1–0 to the Reds*

Love of Liverpool

1

"I love the city and the people here. I've been with them for many years and I fought alongside them."

Bob Paisley

2

"Before, I said that they were maybe the best supporters in England. Now maybe they are the best supporters in Europe."

Rafael Benitez

3

"I may one day leave Liverpool, but Liverpool will never leave me."

Kenny Dalglish

4

"A Liverpool player must play like a lion, give his all. There must be determination, commitment and resolve to be a Liverpool player."

Gerard Houllier

5

"Liverpool's fans are just amazing. The best feeling I have at away games is Anfield. It is just incredible. I love it. You get goose bumps when you see their supporters sing 'You'll Never Walk Alone'."

Arsenal and France star Thierry Henry

1

"We do not expect miracles overnight."

John Henry's message to Brendan Rodgers

2

"I will leave no stone unturned in my quest – and that quest will be relentless – to try and get Liverpool back on the map again as a successful football club."

Brendan Rodgers speaking at his first press conference as Liverpool manager

3

"If he can bring top European football he'll be a king around the place."

John Aldridge speaking shortly after the appointment of Brendan Rodgers as the new Liverpool manager

4

"I'm making this announcement because I don't want the manager to be answering questions when I've already decided what I am going to do."

Jamie Carragher announcing his retirement on 7 February 2013

5

"Jamie Carragher has been a great servant to LFC. Great player and a top fella! Funny guy! Nutter when we were kids, but management material now."

Manchester United's Rio Ferdinand tweeting following Jamie Carragher's decision to retire

CHAPTER

7

EUROPEAN GLORY NIGHTS & THE ONES THAT GOT AWAY

Liverpool Football Club have played more matches in European competition than any other club in England. The Reds have won more games than any other and, more importantly, the trophy cabinet has more silverware and mementoes than any other British club can boast.

The Reds' first venture into European ended in 1965, with a European Cup semi-final defeat in the cauldron that was the Stadio Giuseppe Meazza in Milan; the first final came 12 months later, a heart-breaking defeat at the hands of Borussia Dortmund in the Cup-winners' Cup – the one competition Liverpool failed to win. In 1973, the UEFA Cup came to Anfield for the first of three times and the European Cup followed just four years later.

In this section, you will be able to relive all eight European Cup/UEFA Cup final victories, plus Liverpool's defeat in their first-ever European final, the 1965–66 European Cup-Winners' Cup final and their two losses in the Euopean Cup/UEFA Champions League finals. There is a brief summary of Liverpool's path to these 11 finals, plus a report on the games and full statistical information, dates, venues, crowds, line-ups scorers, etc. And, complementing all of that, in many cases, another snippet of information about the competition has been added, the venue or one of the key characters involved in either the match or the run to the final.

European Cup-Winner's Cup 1965–66

Liverpool qualified for the 1965–66 European Cup-Winner's Cup as FA Cup holders following their 2-1 victory over Leeds United in the 1965 Final. It was only Liverpool's second ever season in European competition, and once again Bill Shankly took them there. The preliminary round of the competition saw Liverpool face the mighty Juventus, which Liverpool won 2-1 over the two legs. Comfortable victories in the first round, 5-2 against Standard Liege of Belgium, and the second round, 2-0 versus Honved of Hungary, saw Liverpool ease into the semi-finals. Glasgow Celtic stood between Liverpool and a place in the final. The first leg was played at Celtic Park, which the home side won 1-0. In the second leg, goals from Tommy Smith and Geoff Strong gave Liverpool a 2-0 win on the night and an overall 2-1 aggregate win. Liverpool found themselves back in the Scottish capital city for the final against Borussia Dortmund at Hampden Park. Siegfried Held put the West German side 1-0 in front after 62 minutes, with Roger Hunt equalising six minutes later. The game ended 1-1 after 90 minutes and went into extra-time, with Reinhard Libuda scoring the winning goal for Germans in the 109th minute.

EUROPEAN CUP-WINNER'S CUP FINAL

5 MAY 1966, HAMPDEN PARK, GLASGOW, SCOTLAND, ATT. 41,000

Borussia Dortmund (0) **1**   **v**   **Liverpool** (0) **1**

Borussia Dortmund won 2-1 after extra time

Held, Libuda   Hunt

Liverpool: Lawrence, Lawler, Byrne, Milne, Yeats, Stevenson, Callaghan, Hunt,

St John, Smith, Thompson

UEFA Cup 1972-73

In the first leg of the 1973 UEFA Cup final, Liverpool crushed their German visitors at Anfield thanks to two goals from Kevin Keegan and a third from Larry Lloyd. Gunter Netzer and his team-mates were simply overwhelmed by the Reds, who played with skill and passion in equally generous quantities. However, in the 65th minute the Reds had a scare, conceding a penalty, but Ray Clemence came to the rescue, saving Jupp Heynckes' kick. In the second leg, two weeks later, Liverpool were on the receiving end of wave after wave of attack from the Germans and went in at half-time 2-0 down, both goals scored by Heynckes. However, in the second half the home side looked like they had burnt themselves out and the Reds held on to claim a 3-2 aggregate victory.

UEFA CUP FINAL

1st LEG

10 MAY 1973, ANFIELD, LIVERPOOL ATT. 41,168

Liverpool (2) **3**	**v**	**Borussia**
Keegan (2), Lloyd		**Moenchengladbach** (0) **0**

Liverpool: Clemence, Lawler, Lindsay, Smith, Lloyd, Hughes, Keegan, Cormack, Toshack, Heighway (Hall), Callaghan

2nd LEG

23 MAY 1973, BORUSSIA-PARK, MOENCHENGLADBACH, WEST GERMANY, ATT. 35,000

Borussia	**v**	**Liverpool** (0) **0**
Moenchengladbach (2) **2**		
Heynckes (2)		

Liverpool: Clemence, Lawler, Lindsay, Smith, Lloyd, Hughes, Keegan, Cormack, Heighway (Boersma), Toshack, Callaghan

UEFA Cup 1975-76

Liverpool won their second European trophy in 1975–76 and just as in 1973, it was the UEFA Cup. The first leg at Anfield was a classic with Liverpool trailing Belgian side FC Bruges 2–0 at half-time. At half-time Bob Paisley brought on Jimmy Case for John Toshack and pushed Kevin Keegan up front. Suddenly the Reds looked more purposeful and three goals in the space of five minutes from Ray Kennedy, Case and Keegan set up an intriguing second leg. The return fixture was a dour affair as Liverpool stifled their stylish Belgian opponents for 90 minutes. In the 12th minute Raoul Lambert scored from the penalty spot to give Bruges the advantage on away goals. However, that position was wiped out with a typical Kevin Keegan strike just three minutes later. The game ended 1–1 and the Reds lifted their second UEFA Cup with a 4–3 aggregate victory.

UEFA CUP FINAL
1st LEG

28 APRIL 1976, ANFIELD, LIVERPOOL, ATT. 49,981

Liverpool (2) **3**   v   **FC Bruges** (2) **2**

Kennedy, Case, Keegan (pen)   Lambert, Cools

Liverpool: Clemence, Neal, Smith, Thompson, Kennedy, Hughes, Keegan, Fairclough, Heighway, Toshack (Case), Callaghan

2nd LEG

19 MAY 1976, JAN BREYDEL STADION, BRUGES, BELGIUM, ATT. 33,000

FC Bruges (1) **1**   v   **Liverpool** (1) **1**

Lambert (pen)   Keegan

Liverpool: Clemence, Neal, Smith, Thompson, Kennedy, Hughes, Keegan, Case, Heighway, Toshack (Fairclough), Callaghan

European Cup 1976-77

Ever since Liverpool first entered European competition in 1964, the club and the fans had dreamed that one day they would win the top prize, the European Cup. In 1976–77 the dream became a reality when Liverpool beat Borussia Moenchengladbach 3–1 in the final in the Stadio Olimpico, Rome, on 25 May 1977. On their way to the final, Liverpool enjoyed aggregate victories over Crusaders, 7–0, Trabzonspor, 3–1, Saint Etienne, 3–2 and, in the semi-final FC Zurich, 6–1. In the final, the only goal of the first half came from Terry McDemott, who burst through the Moenchengladbach defence and ran onto Steve Heighway's diagonal pass, before shooting past Wolfgang Kneib. Alan Simonsen equalised early in the second half, but Liverpool regained the lead with a brilliant header from Tommy Smith. With eight minutes to go, Berti Vogts tripped Kevin Keegen just inside the penalty area and Phil Neal made no mistake from the spot. Liverpool were European champions.

EUROPEAN CUP FINAL
25 MAY 1977, STADIO OLIMPICO, ROME, ATT. 52,000

Liverpool (1) **3**	**v**	**Borussia**
McDermott, Smith,		**Moenchengladbach** (0) **1**
Neal (pen)		Simonsen

Liverpool: Clemence, Neal, Jones, Smith, Hughes, Case, R. Kennedy, Callaghan, McDermott, Keegan, Heighway

DID YOU KNOW THAT?
Phil Thompson was injured before the European Cup final and Tommy Smith, who had planned to retire at the season's end, earned a recall. Smith left Liverpool for Swansea in 1978.

European Cup 1977–78

In 1977–78, Liverpool retained the European Cup without star striker Kevin Keegan who left for SV Hamburg after the 1977 final. However, "The King Is Dead, Long Live The King" was the cry from the Liverpool fans when Kenny Dalglish arrived at Anfield from Celtic at the beginning of the season. Dalglish spearheaded the Liverpool attack throughout the defence of the trophy as Liverpool cruised through the competition. Following a first-round bye, Liverpool beat Dynamo Dresden 6–3 on aggregate in Round Two, SL Benfica 6–2 in the third round and then were paired in the semi-finals with the team they had beaten in the final the previous May – Borussia Moenchengladbach. Liverpool lost the first leg 2–1 in Germany but won 3–0 at Anfield in the return leg. The final, at Wembley Stadium, pitted Liverpool against Belgians FC Bruges. It was a dour, tense affair, but the Reds had Dalglish who grabbed the only goal midway through the second half, set up by another of Bob Paisley's 1977 acquisitions, Graeme Souness.

EUROPEAN CUP FINAL
10 MAY 1978, WEMBLEY STADIUM, ATT. 92,000

Liverpool (0) **1**   v   **FC Bruges** (0) **0**

Dalglish

Liverpool: Clemence, Neal, Thompson, Hansen, Hughes, McDermott, R. Kennedy, Souness, Case (Heighway), Fairclough, Dalglish

DID YOU KNOW THAT?
In their first two European Cup finals, Liverpool faced the two teams they had beaten to win their first two UEFA Cups, Borussia Moenchengladbach and FC Bruges.

European Cup 1980–81

Liverpool's 1980–81 European Cup campaign got off to a poor start when they could only draw 1–1 with Finnish amateurs Oulu Palloseura in their first-round, first-leg encounter in Finland. However, Liverpool won the second leg 10–1. The Reds had much less trouble with Alex Ferguson's Aberdeen, 5–0 on aggregate, and CSKA Sofia, 6–1, in the next two rounds. Bayern Munich, European champions in 1974, 1975 and 1976, were Liverpool's semi-final opponents and they proved difficult to break down. The first leg at Anfield was goalless, but Ray Kennedy scored in Munich and Liverpool progressed to the final on the away goals rule after the match ended 1–1. Europe's most successful club, Real Madrid, were looking for a seventh European Cup when they met Liverpool at the Parc des Princes, in Paris on 27 May. It was far from a classic game and one goal, seven minutes from the end, from Alan Kennedy settled the game. He burst down left wing and fired a shot past Agustin Rodriguez at his near post.

EUROPEAN CUP FINAL

27 MAY 1981, PARC DES PRINCES, PARIS, ATT. 48,360

Liverpool (0) **1**   v   **Real Madrid** (0) **0**

A. Kennedy

Liverpool: Clemence, Neal, Thompson, Hansen, A. Kennedy, Lee, McDermott, Souness, R. Kennedy, Dalglish (Case), Johnson

DID YOU KNOW THAT?

No country can match England's spell of six consecutive European Cup/Champions League final victories from 1977 to 1982. Liverpool led the way with three successes.

European Cup 1983–84

Four the fourth time in eight campaigns, Liverpool ended the season as Europe's champions. BK Odense were brushed aside without difficulty in the first round, but things were much harder thereafter. Ian Rush scored the only goal of the tie, in the second leg of the second round, away to Atletico Madrid, and Benfica shocked the Reds by winning the Anfield leg of the third round, only to be crushed 4–1 at the Stadium of Light. Normal service was resumed in the semi-final as Liverpool recorded 1–0 and 2–1 wins against Dinamo Bucharest to reach the final against AS Roma in their own backyard, the Stadio Olimpico in Rome. Phil Neal gave the Reds the lead after 13 minutes, but Roberto Pruzzo equalised before half-time and there were no more goals, so it went ot a penalty shoot-out. Bruce Grobbelaar's antics in the penalty shoot-out unnerved the Italians, especially Francisco Graziani who fired high over the bar. Liverpool failed once in their five tries and lifted the Cup when Roma had their second failure.

EUROPEAN CUP FINAL

30 MAY 1984, STADIO OLIMPICO, ROME, ATT. 69,693

Liverpool (1) **1**   v   **AS Roma** (1) **1**

Neal   Pruzzo

Liverpool won 4–2 on penalties after extra time

Liverpool: Grobbelaar, Neal, Lawrenson, Hansen, A. Kennedy, Johnston (Nicol), Lee, Souness, Whelan, Dalglish (Robinson), Rush

DID YOU KNOW THAT?

Joe Fagan was Liverpool manager for only two seasons, but he reached the European Cup final in both of them.

European Cup 1984–85

The 1985 European Cup final will always be marred by the truly awful events that unfolded in the Heysel Stadium, Brussels, prior to kick-off that late May night, as 39 fans lost their lives when a wall collapsed. Back in the autumn of 1984, though, Liverpool had begun their defence of the European Cup with home and away wins over Lech Poznan for a 5–0 aggregate score in Round One. In the second round Liverpool faced Benfica in the competition for the second successive year and squeezed through 3–2 on aggregate. Austrian champions Austria Vienna were disposed of 5–2 in the third round, and in the semi-finals Liverpool beat Greece's Panathinaikos 4–0 at Anfield and 1–0 in Athens. At Heysel in the final, Liverpool went down 1–0 to Juventus, the only goal a Michel Platini penalty after Zbigniew Boniek was fouled, but the result pales into insignificance alongside the human tragedy that took place.

EUROPEAN CUP FINAL
29 MAY 1985, HEYSEL STADIUM, BRUSSELS, ATT. 58,000

Liverpool (0) **0**   v   **Juventus** (0) **1**

Boniek (pen)

Liverpool: Grobbelaar, Neal, Beglin, Lawrenson (Gillespie), Hansen, Nicol, Dalglish, Whelan, Wark, Rush, Walsh (Johnson)

DID YOU KNOW THAT?
Heysel was completely rebuilt after the disaster and is Belgium's main football stadium with a 50,000 capacity. It was renamed the King Badouin Stadium and hosted the 1996 European Cup winners' Cup final and matches in Euro 2000.

UEFA Cup 2000–01

On 17 May 2001, Liverpool ended a barren 17 years without European success when they beat the unfancied Spanish side, Alaves, 5–4 in a thrilling UEFA Cup Final. The match got off to a flyer as the Reds cruised into a 2–0 lead thanks to goals from Marcus Babbel and Steven Gerrard inside the first 16 minutes. Esnal, the coach of Alaves, brought on striker Alonso who immediately pulled a goal back for the Spaniards. However, the Reds then scored their third goal against the run of play when Gary McAllister converted a penalty after Michael Owen had been brought down. In the second half the Spanish side threw everything at the Reds and two quick goals from Jaime Moreno levelled the match at 3–3. Gerard Houllier then brought on Vladimir Smicer, Robbie Fowler and Patrik Berger and it was Fowler who restored the Reds' lead with a superb goal in the 73rd minute. Two minutes from time Jordi Cruyff scored to send the game into extra time, a period that saw the Spanish side reduced to nine men. Liverpool won the game on the golden goal rule when Geli scored an own goal in the 116th minute.

UEFA CUP FINAL

17 MAY 2001, WESTFALENSTADION, DORTMUND, GERMANY, ATT. 65,000

Liverpool (3) **5** v **Alavés** (1) **4**

Babbel, Gerrard,   Alonso, Moreno (2),

McAllister (pen), Fowler,   Cruyff

Geli (o.g.)

After extra time

Liverpool: Westerveld, Babbel, Henchoz (Smicer), Hyypia, Carragher, Gerrard, Hamann, McAllister, Murphy, Owen (Berger), Heskey (Fowler)

UEFA Champions League 2004–05

Liverpool's triumph in a penalty shoot-out over AC Milan in the 2005 UEFA Champions League final was one of the greatest comebacks in the competition's much-storied history. Their march to the final began in August 2004 with a third qualifying round win over AK Graz and, on the way to Turkey, they overcame AS Monaco, Olympiakos, Deportivo La Coruna, Bayer Leverkusen, Juventus and finally Chelsea in the semi-finals. In Istanbul's Ataturk Stadium, Liverpool appeared down and out at half-time, trailing 3–0 to AC Milan. Paolo Maldini scored after one minute and Hernan Crespo added two more just before the break. However, three goals in six spectacular second-half minutes, from Steven Gerrard, Vladimir Smicer and Xabi Alonso snatched back the initiative. The game ended 3–3, after extra time, resulting in a penalty shoot-out which Liverpool won 3–2, when Jerzy Dudek saved from Andriy Shevchenko.

UEFA CHAMPIONS LEAGUE FINAL

25 MAY 2005, ATATURK STADIUM, ISTANBUL, ATT. 60,000

Liverpool (0) **3**	v	**AC Milan** (3) **3**
Gerrard, Smicer, Alonso		Maldini, Crespo (2)

After extra time

Liverpool won 3–2 on penalties

Liverpool: Dudek, Finnan (Hamann), Hyypia, Carragher, Traore, Kewell (Smicer 23), Alonso, Gerrard, Riise, Garcia, Baros (Cisse 85)

DID YOU KNOW THAT?
Liverpool became the first English club to keep the trophy in perpetuity.

UEFA Champions League 2006–07

Liverpool's attempt to become European champions for the sixth time came up just short in Athens' Olympic Stadium. For the second time in three seasons, the Reds faced AC Milan, already six-times winners of the European Cup/Champions League. The match was almost a mirror image of the game in Istanbul two years earlier. Then, in the eyes of most neutrals, the Reds had been rather fortunate winners, despite the miraculous second half comeback. This time it was Liverpool who were the better team for most of the 90 minutes, but the result went against them. The game had few clear-cut chances, but when opportunities came their way, Liverpool's finishing let them down. Kaka's free-kick, deflected home by Pippo Inzaghi, on the stroke of half-time gave the *Rossoneri* the lead and Inzaghi's second goal, after 78 minutes, proved too steep a hill for the Reds to climb. Dirk Kuyt pulled a goal back in the last few minutes but, this time, the AC Milan defence held out until the final whistle.

UEFA CHAMPIONS LEAGUE FINAL
23 MAY 2007, OLYMPIC STADIUM, ATHENS, ATT. 74,000

Liverpool (0) **1**   **v**   **AC Milan** (1) **2**

Kuyt   F. Inzaghi (2)

Liverpool: Reina, Finnan (Arbeloa 88), Carragher, Agger, Riise, Pennant, Alonso, Mascherano (Crouch 78), Zenden (Kewell 59), Gerrard, Kuyt

DID YOU KNOW THAT?
Liverpool's seven substitutes came from seven countries: Jerzy Dudek (Poland), Alvaro Arbeloa (Spain) Sami Hyypia (Finland), Harry Kewell (Australia), Mark Gonzalez (Chile), Peter Crouch (England) and Craig Bellamy (Wales).

Liverpool in Europe – Milestone Goals

Liverpool first entered European club football in season 1964–65 and participated in the European Cup. The 2010–11 season was Liverpool's 40th in Europe and in those years the club has scored a grand total of 585 goals. Here are some of the milestone strikes along the way:

1st goal: **Gordon Wallace** v KR Reykjavik, European Cup, first round first leg (A), 17 August 1964

50th goal: **Roger Hunt** v TSV Munchen, Inter Cities Fairs Cup, second round, first leg (H), 7 November 1967

100th goal: **Steve Heighway** v Dynamo Berlin, UEFA Cup, third round second leg (H), 13 December 1972

150th goal: **Jimmy Case** v FC Bruges, UEFA Cup Final, first leg (H), 28 April 1976

200th goal: **Emlyn Hughes** v Anderlecht, European Super Cup, home leg, 19 December 1978

250th goal: **Alan Kennedy** v JK Helsinki, European Cup, second round second leg (H), 2 November 1982

300th goal: **Dean Saunders** v FC Tirol, UEFA Cup, third round second leg (H), 11 December 1991

350th goal: **Nick Barmby** v Rapid Bucharest, UEFA Cup, first round first leg (A), 14 September 2000

400th goal: **Emile Heskey** v Spartak Moscow, UEFA Champions League, group stage (H), 2 October 2002

450th goal: **Djibril Cisse** v TNS CL, UEFA Champions League, qualifying round first leg (A), 19 July 2005

500th goal: **Yossi Benayoun** v Besiktas, UEFA Champions League, group stage (H), 6 November 2007

550th goal: **Ryan Babel** v Olympique Lyonnais, UEFA Champions League, group stage (A), 4 November 2009

SING YOUR HEARTS OUT
FOR THE LADS

The atmosphere at Anfield Stadium, from the 1960s to the 1980s especially, was absolutely unique in world football. There were tens of thousands of fans packed into the ground, with the most fervent of these shoe-horned into the Kop end, the noise that emanated could turn the bravest of men into a gibbering wreck.

And when the Kop started to sing "You'll Never Walk Alone," their red scarves held high above their heads, it was a sight to behold. No wonder, Liverpool enjoyed such a massive home advantage! No Reds player dared to put in a bad performance, not in front of such vocal, passionate support. You never heard of the "Stamford Bridge roar", the "Highbury roar" or the "Goodison roar", but the "Anfield roar": everyone knew it, and if you were a visiting player, you were afraid of it.

This section is all about the songs that Liverpool fans sing, not to taunt their opponents, but to praise their heroes. How important is singing to Anfield faithful? The answer can be found on the famous Shankly Gates at the Stadium. Part of the ironwork of the memorial the greatest of all Liverpool managers is the line, "You'll Never Walk Alone." This anthem, the best known in world football, is one of nine songs to learn. Most are timeless classics and when you sit at Anfield and the crowds starts to sing, you can join in and be part of one of the world's largest and most passionate choirs.

You'll Never Walk Alone

> When you walk through a storm
> Hold your head up high
> And don't be afraid of the dark
> At the end of the storm
> Is a golden sky
> And the sweet silver song of a lark
>
> Walk on through the wind
> Walk on through the rain
> Tho' your dreams be tossed and blown
> Walk on, walk on
> With hope in your heart
> And you'll never walk alone
> You'll never walk alone

Repeat both verses

DID YOU KNOW THAT?

"You'll Never Walk Alone" is probably the world's best known football anthem, but it's origins are far removed from sport. The lyrics were penned by Oscar Hammerstein and music was composed by Richard Rodgers for their famous 1945 Broadway (New York) musical, *Carousel*. It is first sung in the second act, by Nettie Fowler, to Julie Jordan to comfort her after her husband, Billy Bigelow dies in a failed robber, then is reprised in the show's finale.

The Fields of Anfield Road

(to the tune of "The Fields of Athenry")

Outside the Shankly Gates
I heard a Kopite calling:
Shankly they have taken you away
But you left a great eleven
Before you went to heaven
Now it's glory round the Fields of Anfield Road

Chorus:
All round the Fields of Anfield Road
Where once we watched the King Kenny play (and he could play)
Stevie Heighway on the wing
We had dreams and songs to sing
Of the glory round the Fields of Anfield Road

Outside the Paisley Gates
I heard a Kopite calling
Paisley they have taken you away
You led the great 11
Back in Rome in 77
And the redmen they are still playing the same way

All round the Fields of Anfield Road
Where once we watched the King Kenny play (and he could play)
Stevie Heighway on the wing
We had dreams and songs to sing
Of the glory round the Fields of Anfield Road

We All Live in a Red and White Kop

On a Saturday afternoon
We support a team called Liverpool
And we sing until we drop
On the famous Spion Kop

We all live in a red and white Kop
A red and white Kop
A red and white Kop
We all live in a red and white Kop
A red and white Kop
A red and white Kop

(Repeat)

The 12 days of Liverpool

On the 12th day of Christmas my true love gave to me
12 David Hodgson
11 Graeme Souness
10 Craig Johnston
9 Ian Rush
8 Sammy Lee
7 Kenny Dalglish
6 Alan Hansen
5 Ronnie Whelan
4 Mark Lawrenson
3 Barney Rubble
2 Philip Neal
And Brucie in our goal

Poor Tommy Scouser

Let me tell you the story of a poor boy,
Who was sent far away from his home,
To fight for his king and his country,
And also the old folks back home.

So they put him in a highland division,
Sent him off to a far foreign land,
Where the flies swarm around in their thousands,
And there's nothing to see but the sand.

As the battle was starting next morning,
Under the radiant sun,
I remember that poor Scouser Tommy,
Who was shot by an old Nazi gun.

As he lay on the battlefield dyin-dyin-dying,
With the blood gushing out of his head (out of his head)
As he lay on the battlefield dyin-dyin-dying,
These were the last words he said:
Oooh, I am a Liverpudlian,
I come from the Spion Kop,
I like to sing, I like to chant,
I go there quite a lot.

Support a team, that plays in red,
A team that we all know,
A team that we call Liverpool,
To glory we will go.

We won the league, we won the cup,
We've been to Europe too,
We played the Toffees for a laugh,
And left them feeling blue 5–0.

1–2, 1–2–3, 1–2–3–4, 5–0!

Rush scored one,
Rush scored two,
Rush scored three,
And Rush scored four ...

We Won It Five Times

We won it at Wem-b-ely
We won it in Gay Paris
In 77 and 84 it was Rome

We've won it 5 times
We've won it 5 ti-imes
In Istanbul, we won it 5 times

When Emlyn lifted it high
He lit up the Roman sky
Thommo in Paris and Souness
did it as well

We've won it 5 times
We've won it 5 ti-imes
In Istanbul, we won it 5 times

At Wembley we won it our home
Took 26,000 to Rome
20,000 to Paris when we won
it again

We've won it 5 times
We've won it 5 ti-imes
In Istanbul, we won it 5 times

Stevie G's eyes lit up
As he lifted the European Cup
Twenty-one years
And now its coming back
home

We've won it 5 times
We've won it 5 ti-imes
In Istanbul, we won it 5 times
We won it at Wem-b-ely

We won it in Gay Paris
In 77 and 84 it was Rome

We've won it 5 times
We've won it 5 ti-imes
In Istanbul, we won it 5 times

Show Them the Way to Go Home

Show them the way to go home
They're tired and they want to go to bed
Cos they're only half a football team
Compared to the boys in Red

Show them the way to go home
They're tired and they want to go to bed
Cos they're only half a football team
Compared to the boys in Red

Oh Come All Ye Faithful

Oh come all ye faithful
Joyful and triumphant
Oh come ye Oh come ye
To Anfield

Come and behold them
They're the Kings of Europe
Oh come let us adore them Oh
come let us adore them
Oh come let us adore them
Li-i-verpool

Campione

Ooooh Campione,
The one and only,
We're Liverpool,

They say our days are numbered
we're not famous anymore,
But Scousers rule the country
like we've always done before,

Ooooh Campione,
The one and only,
We're Liverpool

CHAPTER

9

THE UPS AND DOWNS
OF LIVERPOOL

Season 2012–13 was the 50th consecutive campaign which Liverpool have enjoyed in the top flight of English football, a current streak bettered by only Arsenal and Everton. It means that this chapter is steeped in history and, hopefully, there will be no need to update it for years to come.

Over the next few pages you will learn about the times when the Reds hit upon hard times and were relegated. But, rather like a lift, what goes down also goes back up and as well as covering the relegation seasons, all of the promotion years are celebrated in a similar fashion. It starts with Liverpool's inaugural season, 1892–93, which although technically not a promotion year, did finish with the club moving up into the Football League and as champions of the Lancashire League.

Each season recorded with a report on Liverpool's progress, details of key matches and the names of the Reds' goalscorers in these games. Together with this there is a full league table for the division and there are also the results of the play-off matches involving Liverpool. No, your eyes are not deceiving you, the Reds did take part in promotion play-offs in their early days. The only difference is that the play-offs in the nineteenth century were called Test Matches and they involved not only clubs trying to go up, but also those fighting to avoid the drop.

Lancashire League 1892–93

Liverpool's first season was spent in the Lancashire League and the opening League game was against Higher Walton, on 3 September 1892, a game Liverpool won 8–0. The line-up was: Sidney Ross, Andrew Hannah (captain), Duncan McLean, Joe Pearson, Joe McQue, James McBride, Tom Wyllie, John Smith, Malcolm McVean, Jonathan Cameron, Arthur Kelvin. McQue, 2, McBride, Smith, 2, McVean and Cameron, 2, scored in the 8–0 victory.

Three teams would dominate the competition Liverpool, Blackpool and Bury. Liverpool and Blackpool finished on 36 points each, with Bury a point behind, and fourth-placed Fleetwood Rangers another 10 behind the Shakers.The title was decided on goal average, and Liverpool's far exceeded the Seasiders', although they did score 18 goals fewer.

Liverpool's first application to join the Football League, in 1892, was rejected but, in 1893, the League decided to expand Division Two and, this time, the Reds' application was successful. Liverpool would not change Leagues again until 1992, when the FA Premier League began.

		P	W	D	L	F	A	Pts
1.	**Liverpool**	22	17	2	3	66	19	36
2.	Blackpool	22	17	2	3	82	31	36
3.	Bury	22	17	1	4	83	24	35
4.	Fleetwood Rangers	22	10	5	7	47	51	25
5.	West Manchester	22	10	4	8	68	55	24
6.	Heywood Central	22	11	1	10	54	60	23
7.	Rossendale	22	8	2	12	46	55	18
8.	Southport Central	22	7	2	13	33	44	16
9.	South Shore	22	5	6	11	46	66	16
10.	Fairfield	22	5	6	11	34	53	16
11.	Nelson	22	4	2	16	54	73	10
12.	Higher Walton	22	3	3	16	28	110	9

Promotion 1893–94

In 1893–94 Liverpool won their first ever League title, the Second Division Championship, just two years after they were formed. And at the end of the season, which was their inaugural campaign in the Football League, they beat Newton Heath (later to become Manchester United) in a promotion/relegation play-off game to clinch promotion to the first division. The pillar of Liverpool's success was their home form – they won all 14 games at Anfield for a maximum 28 points. Their away form was also pretty impressive – Liverpool won eight games and drew six. Thus the Reds were unbeaten all season, scoring 77 goals and conceding just 18. Liverpool's nearest challengers, Small Heath, were eight points behind in second place, and the Reds' two wins over them were significant victories in the race for the title.

		P	W	D	L	F	A	W	D	L	F	A	Pts
1.	**Liverpool**	28	14	0	0	46	6	8	6	0	31	12	50
2.	Small Heath	28	12	0	2	68	19	9	0	5	35	25	42
3.	Notts County	28	12	1	1	55	14	6	2	6	15	17	39
4.	Newcastle United	28	12	1	1	44	10	3	5	6	22	29	36
5.	Grimsby Town	28	11	1	2	47	16	4	1	9	24	42	32
6.	Burton United	28	9	1	4	52	26	5	2	7	27	35	31
7.	Burslem Port Vale	28	10	2	2	43	20	3	2	9	23	44	30
8.	Lincoln City	28	5	4	5	31	22	6	2	6	28	36	28
9.	Woolwich Arsenal	28	9	1	4	33	19	3	3	8	19	36	28
10.	Walsall	28	8	1	5	36	23	2	2	10	15	38	23
11.	Middlesbro' Ironopolis	28	7	4	3	27	20	1	0	13	10	52	20
12.	Crewe Alexandra	28	3	7	4	22	22	3	0	11	20	51	19
13.	Ardwick	28	6	1	7	32	20	2	1	11	15	51	18
14.	Rotherham Town	28	5	1	8	28	42	1	2	11	16	49	15
15.	Northwich Victoria	28	3	3	8	17	34	0	0	14	13	64	9

Test Match (promotion/relegation play-off)

Liverpool	2–0	Newton Heath

Promotion 1895–96

Liverpool made an immediate return to Division One by clinching their second Division Two championship in three years. The Reds' home form again was their key to success, with 14 wins and a draw from their 15 games at Anfield. They scored 65 League goals at Anfield at an average of 4.3 per game. Going into the final match of the season Manchester City needed to beat in Liverpool as both teams boasted 45 points, but Liverpool had the superior goal average. The match ended 1–1 (George Allan), so Liverpool finished on top of the table and they went on to clinch promotion to Division One via success in the end-of-season Test Matches.

		P	W	D	L	F	A	W	D	L	F	A	Pts
1.	**Liverpool**	30	14	1	0	65	11	8	1	6	41	21	46
2.	Manchester City	30	12	3	0	37	9	9	1	5	26	29	46
3.	Grimsby Town	30	14	1	0	51	9	6	1	8	31	29	42
4.	Burton Wanderers	30	12	1	2	43	15	7	3	5	26	25	42
5.	Newcastle United	30	14	0	1	57	14	2	2	11	16	36	34
6.	Newton Heath	30	12	2	1	48	15	3	1	11	18	42	33
7.	Woolwich Arsenal*	30	11	1	3	43	11	3	3	9	16	31	32
8.	Leicester City	30	10	0	5	40	16	4	4	7	17	28	32
9.	Darwen	30	9	4	2	55	22	3	2	10	17	45	30
10.	Notts County	30	8	1	6	41	22	4	1	10	16	32	26
11.	Burton United	30	7	2	6	24	26	3	2	10	15	43	24
12.	Loughborough	30	7	3	5	32	25	2	2	11	8	42	23
13.	Lincoln City	30	7	1	7	36	24	2	3	10	17	51	22
14.	Burslem Port Vale	30	6	4	5	25	24	1	0	14	18	54	18
15.	Rotherham Town	30	7	2	6	27	26	0	1	14	7	71	17
16.	Crewe Alexandra	30	5	2	8	22	28	0	1	14	8	67	13

TEST MATCHES (PROMOTION/RELEGATION PLAY-OFFS)

Liverpool	4–0	Small Heath
Small Heath	0–0	Liverpool
Liverpool	2–0	West Bromwich Albion
West Bromwich Albion	2–0	Liverpool

Promotion 1904–05

Liverpool finished top of Division Two for the third time in 11 seasons, showing just what a yo-yo existence they had led. Bolton Wanderers proved to be the Reds' biggest rivals during the campaign, closely followed by Manchester United. Liverpool lost at both Bolton and United, and drew the return with Wanderders. However, a 4–0 (Jack Cox, Sam Raybould 3) victory over Manchester United at Anfield in the penultimate game of the season ended the visitors' title hopes and Liverpool then won their last League game 3–0 (Jack Parkinson, Robbie Robinson, Cox) against Burnley, also at Anfield, to clinch the Championship by two points from Bolton, and five clear of United. From their 17 home League games, Liverpool notched up 14 wins and three draws, scoring 60 goals and conceding only 12.

	P	W	D	L	F	A	W	D	L	F	A	Pts
1. **Liverpool**	34	14	3	0	60	12	13	1	3	33	13	58
2. Bolton Wanderers	34	15	0	2	53	16	12	2	3	34	16	56
3. Manchester United	34	16	0	1	60	10	8	5	4	21	20	53
4. Bristol City	34	12	3	2	40	12	7	1	9	26	33	42
5. Chesterfield	34	9	6	2	26	11	5	5	7	18	24	39
6. Gainsborough Trinity	34	11	4	2	32	15	3	4	10	29	43	36
7. Barnsley	34	11	4	2	29	13	3	1	13	9	43	33
8. Bradford City	34	8	5	4	31	20	4	3	10	14	29	32
9. Lincoln City	34	9	4	4	31	16	3	3	11	11	25	31
10. West Bromwich Albion	34	8	2	7	29	20	5	2	10	28	28	30
11. Burnley	34	10	1	6	31	21	2	5	10	12	31	30
12. Glossop North End	34	7	5	5	23	14	3	5	9	14	32	30
13. Grimsby Town	34	9	3	5	22	14	2	5	10	11	32	30
14. Leicester Fosse	34	8	3	6	30	25	3	4	10	10	30	29
15. Blackpool	34	8	5	4	26	15	1	5	11	10	33	28
16. Burslem Port Vale	34	7	4	6	28	25	3	3	11	19	47	27
17. Burton United	34	7	2	8	20	29	1	2	14	10	55	20
18. Doncaster Rovers	34	3	2	12	12	32	0	0	17	11	49	8

Relegation 1953–54

Liverpool's 48-year stay in the top division came to an end in 1954 as the club was relegated. Scoring goals, especially at home, was not a problem and their 49 was only two less than runners-up West Bromwich Albion achieve. Unfortunately, away from Anfield, Potsmouth won fewer than Liverpool's two games and their tally of six points on their travels was the worst in the division. The Reds relegation was confirmed some time before the final game and, when all was said and done, Liverpool were bottom of the table, two points behind Middlesbrough but, more importantly, five away from Sheffield United in 20th place.

		P	W	D	L	F	A	W	D	L	F	A	Pts
1.	Wolverhampton Wands	42	16	1	4	61	25	9	6	6	35	31	57
2.	West Bromwich Albion	42	13	5	3	51	24	9	4	8	35	39	53
3.	Huddersfield Town	42	13	6	2	45	24	7	5	9	33	37	51
4.	Manchester United	42	11	6	4	41	27	7	6	8	32	31	48
5.	Bolton Wanderers	42	14	6	1	45	20	4	6	11	30	40	48
6.	Blackpool	42	13	6	2	43	19	6	4	11	37	50	48
7.	Burnley	42	16	2	3	51	23	5	2	14	27	44	46
8.	Chelsea	42	12	3	6	45	26	4	9	8	29	42	44
9.	Charlton Athletic	42	14	4	3	51	26	5	2	14	24	51	44
10.	Cardiff City	42	12	4	5	32	27	6	4	11	19	44	44
11.	Preston North End	42	12	2	7	43	24	7	3	11	44	34	43
12.	Arsenal	42	8	8	5	42	37	7	5	9	33	36	43
13.	Aston Villa	42	12	5	4	50	28	4	4	13	20	40	41
14.	Portsmouth	42	13	5	3	53	31	1	6	14	28	58	39
15.	Newcastle United	42	9	2	10	43	40	5	8	8	29	37	38
16.	Tottenham Hotspur	42	11	3	7	38	33	5	2	14	27	43	37
17.	Manchester City	42	10	4	7	35	31	4	5	12	27	46	37
18.	Sunderland	42	11	4	6	50	37	3	4	14	31	52	36
19.	Sheffield Wednesday	42	12	4	5	43	30	3	2	16	27	61	36
20.	Sheffield United	42	9	5	7	43	38	2	6	13	26	52	33
21.	Middlesbrough	42	6	6	9	29	35	4	4	13	31	56	30
22.	**Liverpool**	42	7	8	6	49	38	2	2	17	19	59	28

Promotion 1961-62

After eight seasons in the wilderness of the Second Division, Bill Shankly led Liverpool to the Division Two Championship title in 1961–62. This fourth second-tier title was the catalyst for an unparalleled period of success. Shankly guided Liverpool to third place in Division Two in both 1959–60 and 1960–61 and built a side that scored freely and defended doggedly. In 21 home League games in 1961–62, Liverpool won 18 and drew three, scoring 68 goals. Their nearest challengers, Leyton Orient, finished a distant eight points behind Liverpool, although they did draw both games against them.

		P	W	D	L	F	A	W	D	L	F	A	Pts
1.	**Liverpool**	42	18	3	0	68	19	9	5	7	31	24	62
2.	Leyton Orient	42	11	5	5	34	17	11	5	5	35	23	54
3.	Sunderland	42	17	3	1	60	16	5	6	10	25	34	53
4.	Scunthorpe United	42	14	4	3	52	26	7	3	11	34	45	49
5.	Plymouth Argyle	42	12	4	5	45	30	7	4	10	30	45	46
6.	Southampton	42	13	3	5	53	28	5	6	10	24	34	45
7.	Huddersfield Town	42	11	5	5	39	22	5	7	9	28	37	44
8.	Stoke City	42	13	4	4	34	17	4	4	13	21	40	42
9.	Rotherham United	42	9	6	6	36	30	7	3	11	34	46	41
10.	Preston North End	42	11	4	6	34	23	4	6	11	21	34	40
11.	Newcastle United	42	10	5	6	40	27	5	4	12	24	31	39
12.	Middlesbrough	42	11	3	7	45	29	5	4	12	31	43	39
13.	Luton Town	42	12	1	8	44	37	5	4	12	25	34	39
14.	Walsall	42	11	7	3	42	23	3	4	14	28	52	39
15.	Charlton Athletic	42	10	5	6	38	30	5	4	12	31	45	39
16.	Derby County	42	10	7	4	42	27	4	4	13	26	48	39
17.	Norwich City	42	10	6	5	36	28	4	5	12	25	42	39
18.	Bury	42	9	4	8	32	36	8	1	12	20	40	39
19.	Leeds United	42	9	6	6	24	19	3	6	12	26	42	36
20.	Swansea Town	42	10	5	6	38	30	2	7	12	23	53	36
21.	Bristol Rovers	42	11	3	7	36	31	2	4	15	17	50	33
22.	Brighton & Hove A.	42	7	7	7	24	32	3	4	14	18	54	31

CHAPTER

10

LIVERPOOL SUPPORTER'S QUIZ

Over the next ten pages, prepare to undergo the sternest test of your Liverpool devotion. Here are ten quizzes, perfect for a trip down to Birmingham or London to watch the Reds pick up three more points. Each round contains 20 questions, all on about Liverpool, club, players, transfers, managers and matches.

Nine of the ten rounds encompass a particular era, mainly a decade, with the other devoted those great European nights which ended with the Liverpool captain holding aloft a piece of European silverware, either the European Cup/Champions League, UEFA Cup/Europea League or UEFA Super Cup. Let's face no other club in England can come close to matching the material available for this round!

You may be quite new to supporting Liverpool, in which case many of the names here will be barely known. But don't worry, you may well have read about the heroes, legends and great moments in stories and features earlier in this book, so if you're doing the quiz on your own, you can cheat and no one will know.

If you're really keen, you can use this section to organise a pub quiz for your Liverpool supporting friends. These rounds of questions are absolutely perfect for this, especially as the answers to all 200 questions can be found at the end of the section.

Quiz 1: The early years

1 Which club called Anfield home before Liverpool FC?

2 Who was the first chairman of Liverpool FC?

3 In which League did Liverpool first play?

4 In which year was the club formed?

5 Which club joined the Football League at the same time as Liverpool?

6 Who did Liverpool beat in a Test match to win promotion at the end of their first season?

7 Who was guest of honour at Liverpool's first FA Cup final?

8 What was the nickname given to Liverpool when they first started playing?

9 Who were Liverpool's first opponents in a competitive match in 1892?

10 Who captained Liverpool's first League championship team?

11 Who was Liverpool's first manager?

12 How many of Liverpool's team in the club's first ever competitive match were Scotsmen?

13 After how many seasons were Liverpool elected to the Football League?

14 When did Liverpool score a club-record 106 League goals?

15 How many League matches did Liverpool lose in the first season in Division Two?

16 Which ground staged Liverpool's first FA Cup final?

17 When were Liverpool League champions for the first time?

18 In which war was the Battle of Spion Kop after which the home end at Anfield was named?

19 Who were Liverpool's first Football League opponents?

20 Who was manager of Liverpool's first Football League championship team?

Quiz 2: The 1920s

1 How often did Liverpool win the League title in the 1920s?
2 Who was the first Anfielder to be made England captain?
3 Which Yorkshire club ended Liverpool's FA Cup run in 1920?
4 Which long-serving Scot scored for Liverpool from inside his own half at West Ham in 1926?
5 For which country did Elisha Scott make most of his international appearances?
6 Which 100-goal Liverpool forward joined Everton in 1927?
7 In which year was the pre-World War II Merseyside derby record crowd of 65,537 set?
8 What was sunny-dispositioned Harry Chambers' nickname?
9 What was the first name of former manager Mr Ashworth?
10 At what position did Tom Bromilow make most of the 300+ appearances for Liverpool?
11 Who were bottom when the Reds topped the table in 1922?
12 How many points above the drop zone did Liverpool finish in 1928 when they were 16th in the table?
13 Who played for Liverpool in their first season and managed the Reds to a 1920s League title?
14 Who won League titles with Liverpool and Everton?
15 In which was the first season when both Merseyside derby League games ended in draws?
16 How many times did Liverpool score five goals at Anfield in the 1922–23 championship season?
17 What was Liverpool's FA Cup run in the 1920s?
18 What role, other than that of manager did George Patterson fulfil in the 1920s?
19 When Sunderland were runners-up to Liverpool for the League title, how many points behind were they?
20 In which position did Elisha Scott play?

Quiz 3: The 1930s

1 How many times did Liverpool finish the First Division's top ten in the 1930s?

2 Who was the first Liverpool manager not to win any titles?

3 Who was the first man to score more than 200 Liverpool goals?

4 True or false? 1930s Reds Cyril and Robert Done were twins.

5 Who was Liverpool's last captain before World War II?

6 To which West Country club did Liverpool pay a £5,000 transfer fee for Phil Taylor in 1937?

7 What was the first name of "Nivvy" Nieuwenhuys?

8 By what score did Liverpool win at Yeovil in 1935?

9 Which future Liverpool manager was signed from Bishop Auckland in 1939?

10 From which club did Liverpool sign former England captain Ernie Blenkinsop in 1934?

11 Who scored a hat-trick in the 7–4 win over Everton in 1933?

12 Why did Bill Jones have to wait eight years for his Reds debut after signing as an 18-year-old?

13 In which round of the 1938–39 FA Cup did Wolverhampton Wanderers beat Liverpool 4–1?

14 After how many seconds did Jack Balmer open the scoring against Everton in February 1938?

15 Who made his last of 341 League appearances in 1932?

16 How many matches did Liverpool play in 1939–40 before the season was cancelled?

17 Ted who scored twice on his debut in 1931, but and never again in 104 more appearances?

18 In which year did George Kay become Reds manager?

19 Gordon Hodgson won one amateur cap for which country?

20 In the January of which year in the 1930s did Liverpool beat Everton 6–0 at Goodison Park?

Quiz 4: The 1940s & 1950s

1 Liverpool's most embarrassing FA Cup exit came in 1959, against which Southern League club?

2 Which club did Bill Shankly leave to take over at Liverpool?

3 Who were Liverpool's first opponents in the 1945–46 FA Cup?

4 By how many points did Liverpool beat Manchester United to win the 1946–47 League title?

5 When did Liverpool play at Wembley for the first time?

6 Which tee-total Liverpool star had a forename Beveridge?

7 Which Alan made the first of his almost 400 Liverpool appearances in February 1953?

8 Who was manager when Liverpool were champions in 1947?

9 Which club was relegated with Liverpool in 1954?

10 For which country did Billy Liddell play?

11 By what score did Liverpool beat Everton in the 1949–50 Merseyside derby FA Cup semi-final?

12 What was Liverpool's worst finishing position in the Second Division in the 1950s?

13 In which League did the Reds play in 1945–46, before the League Championship resumed?

14 Dean Saunders' father played for Liverpool in the 1950s. What was his first name?

15 In what position did Laurie Hughes play?

16 True or false: A 2–1 defeat for Stoke City on 14 June 1947 gave Liverpool the League title.

17 Who did Liverpool beat 7–4 in Billy Liddell's first-team debut?

18 Who scored all five goals in Liverpool's 5–3 Division Two defeat of Bristol Rovers in 1954?

19 Who succeeded George Kay as Liverpool manager?

20 How old was Ronnie Moran when he made his Liverpool debut in 1952?

Quiz 5: The 1960s

Quiz 6: The 1970s

1 From which club did Liverpool sign Emlyn Hughes?
2 What bone did Gerry Byrne break in the 1965 FA Cup final?
3 How many Scotland caps did Ron Yeats win at Liverpool?
4 True or False: Liverpool won the 1962 Division Two title, eight points clear of Leeds United?
5 Who paid Liverpool £31,000 to sign Roger Hunt in 1969?
6 Which club ended Liverpool's first European Cup run?
7 Roger Hunt and which other player scored at least 100 Liverpool goals in the 1960s?
8 Which future England player did Bill Shankly buy from Preston North End in August 1960?
9 Who scored a hat-trick against Newcastle in August 1967, his first goals for Liverpool?
10 In which year did Ian Callaghan make his England debut and Liverpool beat Everton in the Charity Shield?
11 Who was Liverpool's first-choice No.1 for most of the 1960s?
12 Who, in 1965, becameLiverpool's first ever used substitute?
13 Which Peter was an ever-present in the 1964 League championship side?
14 On which ground did Liverpool play their first European final?
15 Who did Liverpool beat in the 1965 FA Cup run, but lose to in the 1966 third round?
16 Which Leeds United goalkeeper threw ball into his own net at the Kop end in 1967?
17 Which full-back scored more than 30 goals for the Reds in the 1960s?
18 Who won titles with Rangers in 1961 and Liverpool in 1964?
19 Who scored 15 goals in 20 League matches in 1963–64?
20 Which 1965 Fa Cup-winner was never on the losing side in 18 career appearances at Wembley?

Quiz 6: The 1970s

1 Who captained Liverpool, England and *A Question of Sport* teams?

2 Who scored Liverpool's equaliser in the 1977 FA Cup Final?

3 Whose final game was Liverpool's first European Cup Final?

4 Who made three Wembley appearances in 1977–78, his first season with Liverpool?

5 Against which Spanish club did "supersub" David Fairclough make a goalscoring debut in 1975?

6 Which was the only team to beat Liverpool at Anfield in the 1972–73 League-winning season?

7 Who grabbed a UEFA Super Cup hat-trick in the 1970s?

8 Which was Bill Shankly's last match as Liverpool manager?

9 Which club knocked out FA Cup holders Liverpool, but as Cup holders lost to the Reds in 1979?

10 Who lifted the League Championship trophy in May 1973?

11 Ian Callaghan, Tommy Smith and who else played in the 1965 FA Cup and 1972 FA Cup tie, both against Leeds?

12 Who joined from Nottingham Forest in 1972 and moved to Bristol City in 1976?

13 Who was an ever-present and won his first title in 1975–76?

14 Who University graduate was nicknamed "Little Bamber"?

15 When did Tommy Smith win his only full England cap?

16 Who scored in both the 1971 and 1974 FA Cup finals?

17 Which boss won six League titles and three European Cups?

18 In which year did Liverpool first do a European trophy and League championship double?

19 Who scored European Super Cup goals for the Reds in 1977 and 1978?

20 Which was the only club to take a point off Liverpool in the last nine games of 1976–77?

Quiz 7: The 1980s

1 Who was the first Zimbabwean to play in an FA Cup Final?

2 Who got a hat-trick in a 1982 5–2 defeat of Manchester City?

3 Who did Liverpool beat in two 1980s FA Cup finals?

4 In July 1987 for which player did Liverpool splash out a club record transfer fee of £1.8 million?

5 By what score did the Reds beat Crystal Palace at Anfield in 1989?

6 How many League Cups did Liverpool win in the 1980s?

7 Who made 492 appearances for the Reds in the 1980s?

8 Who did Graeme Souness replace as captain in 1982–83?

9 Who, in 1989, became the first Liverpool player aged over 30 to score in an FA Cup Final?

10 Which England star cost Liverpool £900,000 in June 1987?

11 Which midfielder scored a hat-trick in successive rounds of the League Cup in 1986?

12 Which ex Anfield hero led Swansea to a League win in 1982?

13 Whose 295-game (with 19 goals) Liverpool playing career ended in August 1986?

14 Who beat Liverpool in a 1986 League Cup semi-final?

15 Which Liverpool player was Scotland captain at the 1982 World Cup?

16 In which city did Liverpool win the 1981 European Cup?

17 Three goalkeepers from which club let in goals in a game against Liverpool in September 1982?

18 In September 1987, which Scotsman scored a hat-trick for Liverpool at Newcastle United?

19 When Liverpool beat Everton 5–0 in 1982–83, who scored four of the goals?

20 Who joined Liverpool from the Vancouver Whitecaps for £250,000 in March 1981?

Quiz 8: The 1990s

1 Who was the 1998 BBC Sports Personality of the Year?

2 Who scored the first ever Premiership goal against Liverpool?

3 Which former Anfield legend played for Newcastle in the 4–3 Liverpool wins in 1996 and 1997?

4 Who lost to Liverpool in the season finale but still clinched the Premier League title that day?

5 Which former Nottingham Forest player scored twice for Liverpool on his debut in 1993?

6 Against which club did Robbie Fowler net his 100th Liverpool goal, in his 165th game, in 1996?

7 With whom did Gerard Houllier become joint boss in 1998?

8 In 1992, who scored in his third FA Cup final for Liverpool?

9 From which club did Liverpool sign David James in 1992?

10 Who left Anfield in 1999, after 139 appearances in ten years?

11 Who was Liverpool's first Premier League captain?

12 Which South African-born German joined from Karlsruhe and left for Stuttgart in 1998–99?

13 Which Arsenal 'keeper let in four goals at Anfield in 1998?

14 Who joined Liverpool from Arsenal in December 1991, after breaking the Reds' hearts in 1989?

15 Which ex-Chelsea striker scored for Liverpool against them at Stamford Bridge in May 1991?

16 In four days in October 1995, how many goals did Liverpool score against Manchester City?

17 Layton who scored against Hull City in his only Reds first-team appearance in September 1999?

18 Who took temporary charge of the team in spring 1992?

19 From which club did Liverpool sign Don Hutchison in 1990?

20 How many times were Liverpool in 1990s League Cup finals?

Quiz 9: The 2000s

1 Who moved from Everton to Liverpool in July 2000?
2 Who, in March 2000, celebrated his 100th Liverpool appearance by scoring with a penalty?
3 Who was the second Reds star to appear in 100 European ties?
4 Who scored the Reds' goal in the 2007 Champions League final?
5 Which Italian substitute scored in the Reds' 4–0 win against Real Madrid in the 2008–09 Champions League?
6 Who stood in as manager during Gerard Houllier's illness in 2001–02?
7 Whose own goal won the UEFA Cup for Liverpool in 2001?
8 For which club did Darren Purse convert a last minute penalty to force extra time in 2001?
9 What was the aggregate score in the 2005 UEFA Champions League semi-final against Chelsea?
10 Which ex Red was on the first-team coaching staff in 2010?
11 Which two Liverpool players went to 2010 World Cup finals but did not appear in a game?
12 Who made the most Liverpool appearances in 2000–01?
13 From which club did Glen Johnson join Liverpool?
14 Against whom did Steven Gerrard score a 2010 Europa League hat-trick?
15 Which brother of an ex-Reds and England star, was Liverpool reserve team boss in 2009?
16 When Liverpool twice beat Manchester United in 2008–09, how many goals did they score?
17 Who went off in the 2005 Champions League final and on in 2007?
18 Who made a goalscoring Scottish debut in November 2010?
19 Who became Gerard Houllier's No. 2 at Aston Villa in 2010?
20 Which player scored twice on his Premier League debut for Liverpool in a 3-2 win at Bolton in September 2007?

Quiz 10: The 2010s

1 Who was the first player Liverpool signed in 2010 – and how many goals did he score for the club?

2 Who was the Reds' leading goalscorer in the 2011–12 FA Cup?

3 Who did the Reds beat in the 2011–12 League Cup semi-finals?

4 From which club did Liverpool sign Charlie Adam in 2011?

5 Name the two former Reds players who played against Liverpool in the fifth round of the 2011–12 League Cup?

6 Name the Denmark international who left the club in 2011?

7 What nationality is Sebastián Coates?

8 Name the three players who scored for Liverpool in the Carling Cup final penalty shoot-out against Cardiff in 2012.

9 Who did Liverpool beat in the 2011–12 FA Cup semi-finals?

10 Which club did Dirk Kuyt join at the end of 2011–12?

11 Which Russian club finished as runners-up behind Liverpool in the 2012–13 Europa League group stages?

12 Who did Charlie Adam sign for after just one season with the Reds?

13 Who was Brendan Rodgers' first signing as Reds manager?

14 Which former UEFA Cup winners did the Reds play in a 2012–13 pre-season friendly?

15 Who became Liverpool's youngest player in September 2012?

16 Where was England international Raheem Sterling born?

17 Which Liverpool player has two Campeanato Gaúcho winners' medals?

18 Which former Borussia Dortmund, Feyenoord and Real Madrid player joined Liverpool in August 2012?

19 Name the six England players to have won 100 caps?

20 Daniel Sturridge broke a club record by scoring how many goals in his first 13 Premier League games for Liverpool?

Answers

Quiz 1 – The early years

1 Everton. **2** John Houlding. **3** Lancashire League. **4** 1892.
5 Woolwich Arsenal. **6** Newton Heath. **7** King George V.
8 The team of Macs. **9** Higher Walton. **10** Alex Raisbeck.
11 John McKenna. **12** All 11. **13** One. **14** 1895–96. **15** None.
16 Crystal Palace. **17** 1901. **18** The Boer War.
19 Middlesbrough Ironopolis. **20** John Watson.

Quiz 2 – The 1920s

1 Twice. **2** Ephraim Longworth. **3** Huddersfield Town.
4 Donald Mackinlay. **5** Northern Ireland. **6** Dick Forshaw. **7** 1927.
8 Smiler. **9** David. **10** Left-half. **11** Manchester United. **12** Two.
13 Matt McQueen. **14** Dick Forshaw. **15** 1921–22. **16** Four.
17 Quarter-finals. **18** Secretary. **19** Six. **20** Goalkeeper.

Quiz 3 – The 1930s

1 Three. **2** George Patterson. **3** Gordon Hodgson. **4** False (they
weren't related). **5** Matt Busby. **6** Bristol Rovers. **7** Berry. **8** 6–2.
9 Bob Paisley. **10** Sheffield Wednesday. **11** Harold Barton.
12 World War II. **13** Fifth round. **14** 10. **15** Tommy Lucas. **16**
Three. **17** Savage. **18** 1936. **19** South Africa. **20** 1935.

Quiz 4 – The 1940s & 1950s

1 Worcester City. **2** Huddersfield Town. **3** Chester. **4** One. **5** 1950.
6 Billy Liddell. **7** A'Court. **8** George Kay. **9** Middlesbrough.
10 Scotland. **11** 2–0. **12** 11th. **13** Football League (North).
14 Roy. **15** Centre-half. **16** True. **16** True. **17** Chelsea. **18** John
Evans. **19** Don Welsh. **20** 18.

Quiz 5 – The 1960s

1 Blackpool. **2** Collar-bone. **3** Two. **4** False (Leyton Orient
were second). **5** Bolton Wanderers. **6** Inter Milan. **7** Ian St John.
8 Gordon Milne. **9** Tony Hateley. **10** 1966. **11** Tommy Lawrence.
12 Geoff Strong. **13** Thompson. **14** Hampden Park. **15** Chelsea.
16 Gary Sprake. **17** Chris Lawler. **18** Willie Stevenson.
19 Alf Arrowsmith. **20** Roger Hunt.

Quiz 6 – The 1970s

1 Emlyn Hughes. **2** Jimmy Case. **3** Kevin Keegan. **4** Kenny Dalglish. **5** Real Sociedad. **6** Arsenal. **7** Terry McDermott. **8** 1974 FA Cup Final. **9** Ipswich Town. **10** Tommy Smith. **11** Chris Lawler. **12** Peter Cormack. **13** Phil Neal. **14** Brian Hall. **15** 1971. **16** Steve Heighway. **17** Bob Paisley. **18** 1973. **19** David Fairclough. **20** Aston Villa.

Quiz 7 – The 1980s

1 Bruce Grobbelaar. **2** Kenny Dalglish. **3** Everton. **4** Peter Beardsley. **5** 9–0. **6** Four. **7** Alan Hansen. **8** Phil Thompson. **9** John Aldridge. **10** John Barnes. **11** Steve McMahon. **12** John Toshack. **13** Sammy Lee. **14** Queens Park Rangers. **15** Graeme Souness. **16** Paris. **17** Luton Town. **18** Steve Nicol. **19** Ian Rush. **20** Bruce Grobbelaar.

Quiz 8 – The 1990s

1 Michael Owen. **2** Teddy Sheringham. **3** Peter Beardsley. **4** Blackburn Rovers. **5** Nigel Clough. **6** Middlesbrough. **7** Roy Evans. **8** Ian Rush. **9** Watford. **10** Steve Harkness. **11** Mark Wright. **12** Sean Dundee. **13** Alex Manninger. **14** Michael Thomas. **15** David Speedie. **16** Ten (6–0 and 4–0 wins). **17** Maxwell. **18** Ronnie Moran. **19** Hartlepool United. **20** Once.

Quiz 9 – The 2000s

1 Nicky Barmby. **2** Patrik Berger. **3** Steven Gerrard. **4** Dirk Kuyt. **5** Andrea Dossena. **6** Phil Thompson. **7** Geli. **8** Birmingham City. **9** 1–0. **10** Sammy Lee. **11** Pepe Reina and Ryan Babel. **12** Markus Babbel. **13** Portsmouth. **14** Napoli. **15** John McMahon. **16** Six. **17** Harry Kewell. **18** Danny Wilson. **19** Gary McAllister. **20** Milan Baros.

Quiz 10 – The 2010s

1 Maxi Rodriguez (17 goals). **2** Andy Carroll. **3** Manchester City. **4** Blackpool. **5** Raul Meireles and Fernando Torres (Chelsea). **6** Christian Poulsen. **7** Uruguayan. **8** Dirk Kuyt, Stewart Downing, Glen Johnson. **9** Everton. **10** Fenerbahçe. **11** FC Anzhi Makhachkala. **12** Stoke City. **13** Fabio Borini from AS Roma. **14** Bayer 04 Leverkusen. **15** Jerome Sinclair. **16** Kingston, Jamaica. **17** Lucas. **18** Nuri Sahin. **19** Billy Wright, Bobby Charlton, Bobby Moore, Peter Shilton, David Beckham, Steven Gerrard. **20** Ten.

PICTURE QUIZ 1: HALLOWED GROUNDS

A Stadio Olimpico, Rome (1977 and 1984); **B** Wembley Stadium, London (1978); **C** Parc des Princes, Paris (1981); **D** Ataturk Olympic Stadium, Instanbul (2005).

PICTURE QUIZ 2: KOP CHOIR

A Ferry Cross the Mersey; **B** You'll Never Walk Alone; **C** Anfield Rap; **D** Poor Tommy Scouser.

PICTURE QUIZ 3: IT'S A CELEBRATION

A Luis Suarez; **B** Steven Gerrard; **C** Robbie Keane; **D** Craig Bellamy.

PICTURE QUIZ 4: THE ROAD TO RIO

A Martin Skrtel (Slovakia); **B** Daniel Agger (Denmark); **C** Joe Allen (Wales); **D** Glen Johnson (England.

PICTURE QUIZ 5: REMIND YOU OF ANYBODY?

A Skippy (Craig Johnston); **B** Crazy Horse (Emlyn Hughes); **C** The Flying Pig (Tommy Lawrence); **D** Digger (John Barnes).

PICTURE QUIZ 6: MEET THE GAFFER

A Bill Shankly (Preston North End); **B** George Kay (West Ham United); **C** Don Welsh (Charlton Athletic); **D** Bob Paisley (Liverpool).

PICTURE QUIZ 7: THEY SHALL NOT PASS

A Elisha Scott; **B** Ray Clemence; **C** Bruce Grobbelaar; **D** Pepe Reina.

PICTURE QUIZ 8: NEW KID ON THE BLOCK

A Kevin Keegan and Bill Shankly; **B** Kenny Dalglish and Bob Paisley; **C** Fernando Torres and Rafa Benítez; **D** Andy Carroll and Kenny Dalglish.